"Gratitude arises when we bring an open and full presence to our life, and its sweetness is a feeling of homecoming. *The Gratitude Project* is an exquisite and wise inquiry into this beautiful expression of the heart!"

—**Tara Brach**, author of *Radical Acceptance* and
Radical Compassion

"*The Gratitude Project* is a practical and thoughtful exploration of how appreciation can help us find hope and strengthen our most important relationships. Gratitude is a mind-set that does far more than make you feel good; it can help you be your best self, connect with others, and see the good in the world."

—**Kelly McGonigal**, author of *The Joy of Movement* and
The Upside of Stress

"In these difficult times, *The Gratitude Project* is timely and beautiful. It offers marvelous, wise, loving, and scientific ways to uplift and nourish the heart."

—**Jack Kornfield, PhD**, author of *A Path with Heart*

The
GRATITUDE
PROJECT

How the science of thankfulness
can rewire our brains for resilience,
optimism, *and* the greater good

Edited by

JEREMY ADAM SMITH
KIRA M. NEWMAN
JASON MARSH
DACHER KELTNER

New Harbinger Publications, Inc.

Publisher's Note

Distributed in Canada by Raincoast Books

Copyright © 2020 by Jeremy Adam Smith, Kira Newman, Jason Marsh, and
              Dacher Keltner
              New Harbinger Publications, Inc.
              5674 Shattuck Avenue
              Oakland, CA 94609
              www.newharbinger.com

Cover design by Sara Christian; Acquired by Ryan Buresh; Edited by Brady Kahn

Library of Congress Cataloging-in-Publication Data

Names: Smith, Jeremy Adam, 1970- editor. | Newman, Kira, editor. | Marsh, Jason, editor. | Keltner, Dacher, editor.
Title: The gratitude project : how the science of thankfulness can rewire our brains for resilience, optimism, and the greater good / edited by Jeremy Adam Smith, Kira Newman, Jason Marsh, Dacher Keltner, PhD.
Description: Oakland, CA : New Harbinger Publications, Inc., [2020] | Includes bibliographical references.
Identifiers: LCCN 2020009883 (print) | LCCN 2020009884 (ebook) | ISBN 9781684034611 (trade paperback) | ISBN 9781684034628 (pdf) | ISBN 9781684034635 (epub)
Subjects: LCSH: Gratitude.
Classification: LCC BF575.G68 G735 2020 (print) | LCC BF575.G68 (ebook) | DDC 179/.9--dc23
LC record available at https://lccn.loc.gov/2020009883
LC ebook record available at https://lccn.loc.gov/2020009884

Printed in the United States of America

22   21   20

10   9   8   7   6   5   4   3   2   1   First Printing

Contents

Preface

The Greater Good Science Center is unique in its commitment to both science and practice. Based at the University of California, Berkeley, one of the world's leading institutions of research and higher education, we sponsor groundbreaking scientific research into social and emotional well-being. More than that, however, we help people apply this research to their personal and professional lives. Since 2001, we have tried to be at the fore of a new scientific movement to explore the roots of happy and compassionate individuals, strong social bonds, and altruistic behavior—the science of a meaningful life.

In 2014, we launched Expanding the Science and Practice of Gratitude, a multiyear project funded by the John Templeton Foundation. We distributed nearly $4 million in funding to researchers across the country, including university faculty, postdoctoral researchers, and graduate students. Their work broke new ground in the study of gratitude, ranging from how gratitude can benefit our cardiovascular health to the role of gratitude in romantic relationships to the neuroscience of gratitude.

Through this work, we have discovered that gratitude can have a transformative impact on individuals and on our families, neighborhoods, schools, workplaces—and perhaps even nations. Studies have consistently found that people who practice gratitude report fewer symptoms of illness, including depression, and more optimism and happiness. As scientists and journalists describe throughout this book, many of these benefits seem to come to us through the way that gratitude fosters stronger relationships, which are associated with more generous and cooperative behavior.

This book turns that research into tools you can use right now to cultivate gratitude in yourself, the people around you, and the world. In these pages, you'll find essays about the basic science of gratitude, supplemented by shorter pieces that highlight specific scientific findings or that complicate the story we're telling about gratefulness. Some of the essays are by the scientists themselves, about their own gratitude journeys. You'll also encounter some personal essays by ordinary people—and conversations with not-so-ordinary people—who are struggling to be grateful in their own lives.

Not all pieces will be relevant to all readers, but every one of them has something valuable to say about gratitude's transformative impact. We have aimed to capture how gratitude can be leveraged across a variety of contexts, from our personal lives to the organization of the entire world. Finally, at the website for this book, http://www.newhar binger.com/44611, you'll find some research-tested exercises to help you see and appreciate the good things in life—and, beyond that, to help the rest of the world see and appreciate them, too. (See the very back of this book for more details.)

Most of these insights and tips come straight from our online magazine, *Greater Good* (https://greatergood.berkeley.edu), which covers "the science of a meaningful life," and Greater Good in Action (http://ggia.berkeley.edu), a free website that collects the best research-based methods for a happier life.

Thanks so much for picking up this book—and we wish you the best.

PART 1

The Roots and Meaning of Gratitude

In this part of this book, scientists define gratitude and draw from their own research to explore its roots in our behavior, biology, and brains. This information will serve as the basis for everything that comes later in this book.

Researchers define *appreciation* as the act of acknowledging the goodness in life—in other words, seeing the positives in events, experiences, or other people (like our colleagues). That's important, but *gratitude* goes a step further: it recognizes how the positive things in our lives—like a success at work—are often due to forces outside of ourselves, particularly the efforts of other people.

Because gratitude encourages us not only to appreciate gifts but also to repay them (or pay them forward), the sociologist Georg Simmel called it "the moral memory of mankind." As Malini Suchak and other contributors argue in their essays, this is how gratitude may have evolved: by strengthening bonds between members of the same species who mutually helped each other out.

CHAPTER 1

What Gratitude Is and Why It Matters

By Robert Emmons with Jeremy Adam Smith

"Thank you" should be a simple thing to say, polite and uncontroversial. In fact, for many people, that's far from the case.

In a 2015 *New York Times* op-ed, for example, best-selling author Barbara Ehrenreich argued that gratitude is nothing less than a plot to maintain an unjust social order. Indeed, gratitude itself is an expression of privilege:

> Is gratitude always appropriate? The answer depends on who's giving it and who's getting it or, very commonly in our divided society, how much of the wealth gap it's expected to bridge. Suppose you were an $8-an-hour Walmart employee who saw her base pay elevated this year, by company fiat, to $9 an hour. Should you be grateful to the Waltons, who are the richest family in America? Or to Walmart's chief executive, whose annual base pay is close to $1 million and whose home sits on nearly 100 acres of land in Bentonville, Ark.? Grateful people have been habitually dismissed as "chumps," and in this hypothetical case, the term would seem to apply.

Ehrenreich isn't alone. For such a seemingly simple idea—that we should give thanks for the good things in our lives—gratitude excites a surprising amount of hostility from some corners of our society. Gratitude has many layers and levels, nuances and niceties; therefore, we need to understand it not just in the ivory tower and theoretically but on the ground—how it is experienced in the lives of real people constructing lives of meaning and purpose. If we don't understand it, then we cannot understand ourselves or life itself. Gratitude is that fundamental, that foundational.

There are many other myths that have been shattered by the science of gratitude. If you're being taught to be grateful for what you have, goes one line of thinking, then you'll never ask for more. Sometimes, gratitude is seen as a threat to rugged individualism—we should pull ourselves up by our bootstraps, without help from anyone. From that standpoint, gratitude is a weakness, not a strength. There are people who feel gratitude as an insincere social obligation—think of being forced to thank Grandma for a present you don't like. Others worry that gratitude can be used to cover up serious problems in a relationship. There are also barriers to gratitude rooted in social position, as when one gender refuses to be grateful to another, as an expression of power over them. These social inequalities led Ehrenreich to say that gratitude is an inappropriate and even disempowering emotion and behavior for people who are disadvantaged. However, a deeper, more nuanced look at the science reveals that this isn't the case at all. If the worth of gratitude "depends on who's giving it and who's getting it," as Ehrenreich writes, then doesn't it follow that we need more gratitude, not less? Perhaps the problem is not gratitude itself but the unequal distribution of gratitude. Perhaps gratitude can be part of the solution to the problems generated by inequality. Gratitude levels the playing field, because in gratitude, we all realize how much we need each other to provide and secure for us things that we cannot provide and secure for ourselves. None of us is self-made. As many essays in this book argue, based on research, gratitude can actually be a tool to address injustice, by strengthening the bonds of people battling against it and by helping people see what they owe to those around them.

Why can gratitude be counterintuitive? In many cases, gratitude simply runs up against some deeply ingrained psychological tendencies. One is the *self-serving bias*. This means that when good things happen to us, we say it's because of something we did, but when bad things happen, we blame other people or circumstances. Gratitude also goes against our need to feel in control of our environment. Finally, gratitude contradicts the *just-world* hypothesis, which says that we get what we deserve in life. Good things happen to good people; bad things happen to bad people. But it doesn't always work out that way, does it? Bad things happen to good people and vice versa.

We like to think that we are our own creators and that our lives are ours to do with as we please. We take things for granted. We assume that we are totally responsible for all the good that comes our way. After all, we have earned it. We deserve it. A scene from *The Simpsons* captures this mentality. When asked to say grace at the family dinner table, Bart Simpson offers the following words: "Dear God, we paid for all this stuff ourselves, so thanks for nothing." In one sense, of course, Bart is right. The Simpson family did earn their own money. But he is missing the bigger picture. Grateful people sense that much goodness happens independently of their actions or even in spite of themselves. Gratitude implies humility—a recognition that we could not be who we are or where we are in life without the contributions of others. How many family members, friends, strangers, and all those who have come before us have made our daily lives easier and our existence freer, more comfortable, and even possible? It is mind-boggling to consider.

Indeed, contemporary social science research reminds us that we overlook gratitude at our own emotional and psychological peril. After decades of ignoring gratitude—perhaps because it appears, on the surface, to be a very obvious emotion, lacking in interesting complications—researchers have found that gratitude contributes powerfully to human health, happiness, and social connection. The social benefits—which we'll describe later in this book—are especially significant here because, after all, gratitude is a social emotion. It strengthens relationships because it requires us to see how we've been supported and affirmed by other people. This cuts to the very heart of our definition of gratitude, developed by Robert Emmons and adopted by the Greater Good Science Center. By this definition, gratitude has two components. One is an affirmation that there are good things in the world, things from which we've benefited. Two is a recognition of where that goodness comes from—the people and things in our life that have conspired to give it to us.

What Gratitude Is

First, gratitude is an affirmation of goodness. We affirm that there are good things in the world, gifts and benefits we've received. This doesn't mean that life is perfect; it doesn't ignore complaints, burdens, and hassles. But when we look at life as a whole, gratitude encourages us to identify some amount of goodness in our life. It's easy to miss the good, because we simply get used to it. Research shows that our emotional systems like newness. They like novelty. They like change. So, positive emotions tend to wear off quickly. We adapt to positive life circumstances so that before too long, the new car, the new spouse, the new house—they don't feel so new and exciting anymore. But gratitude makes us appreciate the value of something, and when we appreciate the value of something, we extract more benefits from it; we're less likely to take it for granted. In effect, gratitude allows us to participate more fully in life. Instead of adapting to goodness, we celebrate goodness.

The second part of gratitude is figuring out where the goodness in our lives comes from. We recognize the sources of this goodness as being outside of ourselves. It doesn't stem from anything we necessarily did ourselves in which we might take pride. Sure, we can appreciate positive traits in ourselves, but true gratitude involves a humble dependence on others: we acknowledge that other people—or even higher powers, if you're of a spiritual mind-set—have given us many gifts, big and small, to help us achieve the goodness in our lives.

When you're grateful, you have the sense that someone else is looking out for you. Someone else has provided for your well-being; in fact, you might notice a network of relationships, past and present, with people who are responsible for helping you get to where you are right now. Once you start to recognize the contributions that other people have made to your life—once you realize that other people have seen the value in you—it will transform the way you see yourself.

It's this sense of self-worth that opens the door to transforming the world around you.

Why Does Gratitude Matter?

One of the myths concerning gratitude is that it undercuts ambition. If you are grateful, then you'll just be satisfied, complacent, lazy, and lethargic, perhaps passively resigned to an injustice or a bad situation. You'll give up trying to change something. In fact, the opposite appears to be true: gratitude not only doesn't lead to complacency but drives a sense of purpose and a desire to do more.

Studies have found that people are actually more successful at reaching their goals when they consciously practice gratitude. When we ask people to identify six personal goals on which they want to work over the next ten weeks—these could be academic, spiritual, social, or health-related goals, like losing weight—we find that study participants randomly assigned to keep a gratitude journal, once a week recording five things for which they're grateful, exert more effort toward their goals than participants who aren't asked to practice gratitude. In fact, the grateful group makes 20 percent more progress toward their goals than the nongrateful group—and they don't stop there. They report continuing to strive still harder toward their goals.

This finding does not surprise us because people who keep a gratitude journal in our studies consistently report feeling more energetic, alive, awake, and alert. Yet they don't report feeling more satisfied with their progress toward their goals than other people do. They don't become complacent or satisfied to the point that they stop making an effort. This relates to other research showing that gratitude inspires *prosocial* behavior such as generosity, compassion, and charitable giving—none of which suggests passivity or resignation. Instead, it suggests that gratitude motivates people to go out and do things for others—to give back some of the goodness that they recognize receiving themselves. We also have learned that gratitude for health care received is the single biggest factor driving individuals and families to make monetary donations to hospitals (to the tune of $8 billion a year). Generosity is not passivity.

In fact, we (Emmons and colleagues) published a study in *Motivation and Emotion* a few years ago that found that kids who were more grateful than their peers at age ten were by age fourteen performing more prosocial activities—such as volunteering—and feeling greater social integration, meaning that they felt like part of their family and community and experienced a desire to give back. Again, the grateful people didn't show passive resignation; they were out in the world doing stuff to make life better for others. In chapter 6, our contributors will further explore these kinds of benefits in "Why Gratitude Is Good for Us."

Of course, as we're thinking about what gratitude is and why it matters, it's also important to understand what gratitude is *not*. Sometimes, we think about gratitude in ways that diminish our understanding of it. What are some of the myths about gratitude—and what facts and truths do they conceal?

Gratitude Isn't a Naïve Form of Positive Thinking

Some people claim that gratitude is just about thinking nice thoughts and expecting good things—and ignores the negativity, pain, and suffering in life. Well, they're wrong. Consider our definition of gratitude, as a specific way of thinking about receiving a benefit and giving credit to others besides yourself for that benefit. In fact, gratitude can be very difficult, because it requires that you recognize your dependence on others, and that's not always positive. You have to humble yourself, in the sense that you have to become a good receiver of others' support and generosity. That can be very hard—most people are better givers than receivers.

What's more, feelings of gratitude can sometimes stir up related feelings of indebtedness and obligation, which doesn't sound like positive thinking at all: *If I am grateful for something you provided to me, I have to take care of that thing—I might even have to reciprocate at some appropriate time in the future.* That type of indebtedness or obligation can be perceived very negatively—it can cause people real discomfort, as Jill Suttie explores in her essay later in this book, "How to Say Thanks Without Feeling Indebted."

The data bear this out. When people are grateful, they aren't necessarily free of negative emotions—we don't find that they necessarily have less anxiety or less tension or less unhappiness. Practicing gratitude magnifies positive feelings more than it reduces negative feelings. If gratitude were just positive thinking, or a form of denial, you'd experience no negative thoughts or feelings when you're keeping a gratitude journal, for instance. But, in fact, people do.

But when we do experience negative thoughts and feelings, the context in which we experience them changes drastically with gratitude. In moments of adversity, for instance, gratitude helps us see the big picture and not feel overwhelmed by the setbacks we're facing in the moment. Consider a study led by Philip Watkins, published in the *Journal of Positive Psychology*, in which participants were asked to recall an unpleasant, unresolved memory—a time they were victimized or betrayed or hurt in some way that still made them upset. The participants were randomly assigned to complete one of three different writing exercises, one of which involved focusing on positive aspects of the upsetting experience and considering how it might now make them feel grateful. Afterward, the gratitude group reported feeling more closure and less unpleasant emotions than participants who didn't write about their experience from a grateful perspective. The grateful writers weren't told to deny or ignore the negative aspects of their memory, yet they seemed more resilient in the face of those troubles.

Similarly, we asked people suffering from severe neuromuscular disorders to keep a gratitude journal over two weeks. Given that much of their lives involved intense discomfort and visits to pain clinics, we wondered whether the participants would be able to find anything to be grateful for. Yet they not only found reasons to be grateful but also experienced significantly more positive emotions than a similar group who didn't keep a gratitude journal. The gratitude group also felt more optimistic about the upcoming week, felt more connected to others (even though many of them lived alone), and reported getting more sleep each night—an important indicator of overall health and well-being.

Gratitude Is Not a Zero-Sum Game

Some people assume that if you are grateful, you credit others for your own success. In other words, when you recognize the ways others have helped you, you risk overlooking your own hard work or natural abilities.

Research suggests that this is not the case. In one study, researchers administered a purportedly difficult test and told the study participants that they could win money for doing well on the test. Then the participants received a helpful hint that would help them get a high score. All the participants regarded the hint as helpful, but only those who felt personally responsible for their own score felt grateful for the hint. Gratitude was actually associated with a greater sense of personal control over their success.

We have corroborated this in other studies: grateful people give credit to others but not at the expense of acknowledging their own responsibility for their success. They take credit, too. It's not an either/or: *Either I did this all myself or somebody else did it for me.* Instead, they recognize their own feats and abilities while also feeling gratitude toward the people—parents, teachers—who helped them along the way.

Many of these myths—that gratitude is just positive thinking, an empty platitude; that gratitude is just about giving others credit and never taking it yourself; that gratitude is just self-congratulation that leads to complacency; or that gratitude is only appropriate for the privi-leged—spring from a fundamental misconception about gratitude: that it is a simplistic emotion. But part of what has kept researchers inter-ested in gratitude for decades is that it is deceptively complicated; each year we seem to encounter another nuance or layer to it. Once we appreciate these complexities of gratitude, documented by years of sci-entific research, we are in a better position to enjoy all the strengths and goodness it can bring.

Levels of Gratitude

By Summer Allen

Robert Emmons defines gratitude as an affirmation of goodness and of the relationships that bring us goodness. But how do we experience that goodness inside our minds? There is evidence that gratitude can be thought of as an emotional experience with three hierarchical levels: affective trait, mood, and emotion. Affective traits, as defined by psychologist Erika Rosenberg, are "stable predispositions toward certain types of emotional responding." Thus, some people may have a more grateful disposition. Moods, according to Rosenberg, "wax and wane, fluctuating throughout or across days." And emotions are more short-term reactions to particular events—for example, feeling grateful after receiving a gift.

These three levels of gratitude can influence one another. A 2004 study of this hierarchical model of gratitude concluded that "grateful moods are created both through top-down effects (the effects of personality and affective traits), bottom-up effects (the effects of discrete interpersonal and emotional episodes), and the interaction of these effects"—meaning who you are, what you experience, and the way these things play off each other. This study found that grateful moods set the stage for more frequent and pervasive grateful emotions. However, people who were more grateful by nature (with more trait gratitude) were also more emotionally resilient in their everyday lives. Their sense of gratitude was less dependent on particular events.

CHAPTER 2

Looking for Gratitude's Roots in Primates

By Malini Suchak

"Thank you." Two simple words, among the most repeated on a daily basis. When we travel to a foreign country, it is often one of the first phrases we learn, just after "hello." When children start making verbal requests, their parents quickly teach them to say "please" and "thank you."

Studies from neuroscience have identified brain areas that are likely involved in experiencing and expressing gratitude, providing evidence for the idea that gratitude is an intrinsic component of the human experience. Additionally, a few studies have identified specific genes that may underlie our ability to experience gratitude. But if gratitude is so important to human life, where did it come from? How did we as humans end up as a species for whom gratitude is as much a part of our social relationships as gossip?

It turns out the question of the origins of emotion is centuries old, with Darwin himself suggesting that humans and other animals share the "same emotions, even the more complex ones such as jealousy, suspicion, emulation, gratitude, and magnanimity." And—at least for gratitude—some initial research suggests that Darwin might be right.

Searching for Gratitude in Primates

How do you systematically look for evidence of gratitude in species that can't say thank-you? Since you can't ask them how they're feeling, you observe behavior—and the behavior that we researchers believe reflects gratitude is called *reciprocity*. Reciprocity is the exchange of goods and services between two individuals over time, often characterized as "you scratch my back and I'll scratch yours." This kind of mutual arrangement can be beneficial to both parties, making them more likely to survive.

Animals as diverse as fish, birds, and vampire bats engage in "reciprocal altruism" activities—behaviors that one animal performs to help another member of their species, even at a cost to themselves. We often presume animals do this because they recognize, at some instinctual level, that the other individual may repay the favor at a later date. But many scientists see this desire to repay generosity as an expression of gratitude, more so than a calculation. In fact, some scientists suggest that gratitude may have evolved as a mechanism to drive this reciprocal altruism, thereby turning strangers into friends and allies who are more likely to help one another.

This means that reciprocity may have been fundamental in the evolution of gratitude. In humans, with our ability to express our emotions through language, reciprocity and expressions of gratitude often go together. Famed evolutionary biologist Robert Trivers suggests that gratitude is the emotion that regulates our response to altruistic acts by others and motivates our reciprocal response (our response in kind). As researcher Michael McCullough has explained, gratitude is a positive feeling that can alert us to the benefits we've received from others and inspire us to show appreciation—which will in turn make others more likely to help us in the future. In this way, gratitude helps build social bonds and friendships between individuals.

For example, researchers set up an experiment where half of the participants thought they received money from a partner, and the other half thought they received it by chance. In the next round of the study, the participants were given $10 and allowed to divide it up between themselves and their partners. Not surprisingly, individuals who thought their partner had given them money were more likely to distribute money back to their partners than those who thought they had received it by chance. When asked why they donated money, they most often said, "to express appreciation." In this experiment, the participants could not see or interact with their partners, so the only way to express their gratitude was by returning the favor. We may be seeing a very similar phenomenon in some of our closest relatives, the other primates—they can't express gratitude verbally, so returning favors may be the best way for them to do it.

A good deal of evidence suggests that our primate relatives engage in reciprocity in food sharing and other domains. For example, in one study we gave chimpanzees a task that required two chimpanzees to pull in a tray of food. The environment was set up so that the chimpanzees could come and go as they pleased, which meant that one chimpanzee was often sitting there waiting for a partner to arrive. We predicted that passing chimpanzees might choose to help just the chimpanzees they were friendly with—or perhaps the chimpanzees that were the best at solving the task would be most likely to act. Instead, passing chimpanzees were more likely to help a chimpanzee in need of a partner to pull the tray if that chimpanzee had also helped them in the past. Reciprocity seemed more important than friendship and skill in their choices.

Unlike our closer chimpanzee relatives, capuchin monkeys and humans last shared an ancestor approximately 35 million years ago. Capuchins are also highly cooperative. This makes them great subjects to see just how far back we can trace the tendency to engage in reciprocity. In one task, we gave one capuchin monkey a choice between a prosocial option that rewarded themselves and a partner with a treat like a piece of apple and a selfish option that only rewarded the chooser. In this context, they were prosocial about 60 percent of the time.

But when we gave them the opportunity for reciprocity, by alternating the roles of chooser and partner from task to task—so that a partner monkey could become a chooser in turn, with the ability to choose the prosocial option at that point to reward the original chooser—they were significantly more prosocial, now nearly 75 percent of the time. So, the ability to reciprocate—and potentially, to express gratitude—would seem to increase the likelihood of reciprocal, prosocial behavior.

Even more compelling, we found that capuchins are highly attuned to whether a situation is reciprocal or not. In one variation, we didn't actually let the second monkeys choose; we chose for them but mimicked past choices that the second monkeys had made. The first monkeys went back to a level of prosocial behavior similar to when they were the only chooser, suggesting that they can clearly identify when another monkey has helped them and reward that monkey for doing so.

Finally, recent research suggests that capuchin monkeys and four-year-old children engage in upstream reciprocity, or "paying it forward," in a remarkably similar fashion. In upstream reciprocity, receiving a favor makes individuals more likely to donate a favor to someone else in the future. In the case of the monkeys and children, after one individual donated a favor to another, that individual was taken out of the testing area and a new partner brought in. Surprisingly, both the capuchins and the children were more likely to donate a reward to the new partner if they had recently received a reward themselves. They had no opportunity to repay the individual who had rewarded them before but instead chose to pay their good fortunes forward. Some researchers have suggested that gratitude is the motivation behind paying it forward in humans, and this might also be the case in capuchin monkeys.

Gratitude Is a Part of What We Are

We would be remiss not to point out that although it entails high levels of prosocial behavior characteristic of gratitude, reciprocity itself doesn't necessarily have to involve gratitude. It can occur as a transaction achieved by keeping track of benefits given and received and result in feelings of obligation or indebtedness rather than gratitude. However, there is good reason to believe that something else is going on with other primates.

First, if reciprocity were driven by indebtedness rather than gratitude, primates would have to be keeping track of costs and benefits over time. A lot of research has shown, though, that this level of calculation and memory is really not realistic for us or our primate relatives. In reality, reciprocal exchanges are more likely to be driven by emotional responses, which are easier to keep track of. Grateful emotions reinforce the relationship between two individuals, and individuals with close relationships are likely to provide favors for each other in the future, no questions asked.

Further, if you take away the ability to ask people why they are helping, experiments of gratitude in humans look very much like experiments of reciprocity in other species. What is measured is the propensity to return favors, with gratitude as the motivational mechanism proposed to drive that behavior. When the similarities are this great, it becomes difficult to argue that what we see in nonhuman primates is fundamentally different from what we see in humans. We may not be able to ask primates to fill out a survey, but the similarities in how they act are compelling.

All of the research to date uses repayment of favors as the purported way to acknowledge a past favor done. While this is likely the best, most observable measure we have, it is quite different from a verbal thank-you given from one human to another. There may be a subtle expression, gesture, or some other communication that other species use to acknowledge kind acts. The trick will be for us to develop a deep enough understanding of other species' communication systems to discover it.

We've come a long way since Darwin first proposed that gratitude may be a universally experienced emotion. Although we are not yet at the point where we can "speak chimp" well enough to understand chimpanzees' expressions of gratitude, the behavior of our closest relatives certainly suggests that we humans are not alone in the importance we place on gratitude.

We often blame our worst tendencies, like aggression and competition, on our evolutionary history. It's important to remember that some of our most positive qualities, like empathy and gratitude, are also a part of that history. When we discover these traits in our closest relatives, it's a powerful reminder that the "good" in human nature is deeply rooted, as well. The research suggests that, in all likelihood, our propensity for gratitude really does have deep evolutionary roots, and it will be up to us to find out how deep they go.

Do Genes Affect Your Gratitude?

By Summer Allen

In investigating the origins of gratitude, researchers not only consider humans' genetic inheritance from history but also look at our genes in the present. In a study by Michael Steger and colleagues, identical twins (who essentially have the same DNA) reported more similar levels of gratitude than did fraternal twins—who share only 50 percent of their DNA—suggesting that there may be a genetic component to gratitude. Other studies have explored what specific genes may underlie a person's grateful (or less grateful) disposition. One promising candidate is a gene called CD38, involved in the secretion of the neuropeptide oxytocin. A study by Sara Algoe and colleagues found that differences in this gene were significantly associated with the quality and frequency of expressions of gratitude toward a romantic partner in both the lab and in regular daily life.

In one part of this study, for example, members of heterosexual romantic couples noted whether "I thanked my partner for something he/she did that I appreciated" every night for two weeks. Partners with one particular variant of the CD38 gene reported thanking their partners about 45 percent of the time, whereas partners with another variant thanked their partners more than 70 percent of the time. That's a difference of about three and a half days.

Another gene that appears to influence gratitude is a gene called COMT, which is involved in the recycling of the neurotransmitter dopamine in the brain. A recent study by Jinting Liu and colleagues found that people with one version of this gene reported feeling more grateful than people with another version of the gene reported feeling. This result was consistent with the results of an earlier study that found that the brains of people with the less grateful version of the gene showed a greater *negativity bias*—they responded more to fearful faces, as compared to neutral faces, and less to happy faces.

While the less grateful version of the COMT gene isn't all bad—there is evidence it has advantages for memory and attention—the results reported by Liu and colleagues suggest that this gene variant may predispose people to be not only less sensitive to positive life events but also super sensitive to negative life events. They write that "these individuals may gradually form, over the developmental course of life, a habit of neglecting the positive aspects of life events and complaining about misfortunes, resulting in decreased positive personality traits, such as gratitude and forgiveness."

It's important to note two things about these studies. First, they can't tell us anything about how anyone with a particular gene would act or behave on a given day. It isn't as if everyone with one version is walking around constantly feeling blessed while people with the other version are total ingrates. And, second, the genes discussed above are only two out of the possibly hundreds or thousands of genes that could be involved in how we experience a complex emotion like gratitude—besides all the other social factors like religion and culture that are also at play. Emotions are complicated things! These results do suggest, however, that genes may contribute to a person's tendency to be more or less prone to seeing the world through grateful eyes.

CHAPTER 3

How Gratitude Develops in Us
By Maryam Abdullah, Giacomo Bono, Jeffrey Froh, Andrea Hussong, and Kira Newman

As we saw in the previous chapters, gratitude has roots in evolution and biology—and yet it is still a skill that needs to be socially transmitted. Gratitude is not a simple gesture but a rich, multifaceted experience that involves thoughts, feelings, actions—and consequences. Gratefulness doesn't come to us all at once. It's something we need to learn through childhood and adolescence, and it develops over time as our brains grow more sophisticated. As children grow, they are developing the mental building blocks—a web of cognitive, social, and emotional skills—that will eventually allow them to experience gratitude fully. Researchers are beginning to understand what the developmental trajectory of gratitude looks like as we grow into adulthood. Looking at how gratitude develops in us in childhood and adolescence reveals how gratitude evolves from a form of reciprocity to a deep moral value.

The Building Blocks of Gratitude

At three years old, suggests current research, you were already starting to build the foundations of gratitude. In one study, researchers gathered together a group of three-year-olds and tested them on their understanding of emotions. The children were asked to identify feelings like happiness, sadness, anger, and fear in different characters—either faces they looked at or puppets in a story. They also brainstormed the potential causes of an emotion: "The puppet is sad. What made the puppet feel this way?"

In addition, researchers tested how well the three-year-olds understood other people's mental states, including whether they could predict someone else's behavior or thoughts if different from their own. For example, in one of the tests, the researchers showed them a cereal box containing pencils and asked what a buddy of theirs would think is in the box. The researchers also visited the children when they were four years old and gave them the same tests. Then, a year later, when the children were five, the researchers tested the children's understanding of gratitude. The children heard stories where help was given, like an aunt finding her nephew's lost cat or a student lending another student a sweater. They were considered to have a better understanding of gratitude if they realized that the kids who were helped would feel good about the helper (not just good in general), and if they believed the kid should be kind in return.

Ultimately, the children who had greater knowledge of emotions as three-year-olds grew to understand other people's minds better as four-year-olds and had a greater understanding of gratitude as five-year-olds. This means that certain emotional and cognitive skills that we're acquiring as toddlers—mainly an understanding of our own feelings and the ability to perceive other people's—might underpin the development of gratitude. As these skills naturally develop, children are able to move beyond simple thank-yous to the positive thoughts and behaviors that make up genuine gratefulness. As this internal process unfolds, these children are also being affected by what they're experiencing and being taught. Researcher Andrea Hussong and her team at the University of North Carolina at Chapel Hill found that six- to nine-year-olds are more grateful when their parents expose them to environments that might be gratitude-promoting.

Hussong and her team asked one hundred parents whether they deliberately select activities for their child with the goal of helping them develop and express gratitude. For example, parents might choose schools that have a gratitude curriculum, set up playdates or dinners with kids and families who often express thanks, or sign their kids up for service activities that remind them of how fortunate they are. They found that the more parents did this, the more frequently they observed their children showing gratitude.

Parents often make decisions that shape the environments to which their children are exposed, and they select those environments based on a set of sometimes-competing goals. Do you pick sports to foster a healthy body or community service to boost your child's civic engagement? The practice of gratitude, too, can be thought of as a goal. And if parents have a goal of promoting gratitude in their children, they can select situations for their children in which gratitude may arise. For younger children, schools and clubs that provide age-appropriate practices and support children's autonomy will have adults who are better able to connect with the intrinsic interests and preferences of children, which helps establish healthy attachments. For school-age children, it's more about setting up playdates, so children can develop friendships.

Once parents begin structuring environments to foster gratitude in their children, what actually happens? Hussong and her team have also explored what children's early attempts at gratitude look like. They found that parents most often encouraged—and kids most often showed—gratitude through action. Parents prompted them to say thank-you, give a hug, or lend a hand, and they did.

Not all grateful actions are created equal, though, and other research suggests that gratitude becomes more sophisticated as children get older. In 2018, Jonathan Tudge and his colleagues published a series of studies examining how gratitude develops in children in the United States, Brazil, Guatemala, Turkey, Russia, China, and South Korea. First, they asked a group of seven- to fourteen-year-olds, "What is your greatest wish?" and "What would you do for the person who granted you that wish?" Then they grouped the answers into three categories:

- *Verbal gratitude:* Saying thank-you in some way.

- *Concrete gratitude:* Reciprocating with something the seven- to fourteen-year-old would like, such as offering the person some candy.

- *Connective gratitude:* Reciprocating with something the wish-granter would like, such as friendship or help.

As you might expect, children were less likely to respond with concrete gratitude as they got older, whereas younger and older kids expressed verbal gratitude at similar rates, although there were exceptions to these trends. (Brazilian children showed more verbal gratitude as they got older, while concrete gratitude didn't decline with age in Guatemala and China, where it was fairly rare to begin with.) And as children grew older, they expressed more connective gratitude in the United States, China, and Brazil. This type of gratitude builds relationships and more fully takes into account another person's thoughts and feelings.

Four Components of Gratitude

As children grow in their gratitude, they are absorbing behaviors and messages from their caregivers. Children's early experiences of gratitude may focus on tangible behaviors because that's what parents emphasize (and model themselves). But our research suggests that there are three other components of gratitude that take place mostly inside our own heads.

As part of the Raising Grateful Children project, Hussong and her team have explored gratitude experiences with families as their children have grown from kindergarteners to young teens. Based on the scientific literature and conversations with parents, the Raising Grateful Children team has come to think about gratitude as an experience that has four components:

- What we *notice* for which we can be grateful. Part of gratitude is stopping and paying attention when we're given something, and recognizing the good things that already exist in our lives. It also involves seeing the thought and care behind the gifts we receive.

- How we *think* about why we have been given those things. We feel more grateful if we believe a gift was spontaneous and unearned, not something that the giver was obligated to give us. Gratitude may arise when we consider why the giver chose to give this particular gift to us.

- How we *feel* about the things we have been given. The happiness or connection we experience in receiving can translate into grateful feelings.

- What we *do* to express appreciation in turn. Giving a thank-you or a hug can be a way to express the positive feelings we have. Or we might be inspired to pay it forward, giving to others so that they can have the positive experience of receiving.

Older children and adults are more likely to spontaneously engage in all four parts of gratitude, but younger children may only engage in some of these parts and only when prompted. Children may show more gratitude as they gain cognitive skills, practice those skills, and begin to connect the *notice-think-feel* parts of experiencing gratitude with the *do* part of expressing gratitude.

As we noted above, parents have a role to play in helping their kids develop gratitude muscles. In our studies, parents pay a lot less attention to the *notice-think-feel* part of the equation than to the *do*. In fact, a third or fewer parents said that they asked their six- to nine-year-olds about their grateful thoughts or feelings.

But even at a young age, kids are able to learn grateful thought processes. Hofstra University researcher Jeffrey Froh and his colleagues designed lessons on grateful thinking for elementary school students ages eight to eleven, helping them think more deeply about what happens when someone offers help—including the intentions behind it, the costs the helper incurs, and the benefits it provides, all of which guide one's attention to do grateful thinking. Over a series of lessons, students considered examples of nice things that people do for others—like a sibling helping with homework or a friend sharing a snack—and discussed what that experience is like for the helper and the person being helped. The researchers found that students who practiced grateful thinking indeed felt more thankful and appreciative—and also wrote more thank-you cards when given the opportunity.

Studies like these emphasize that gratitude is not just about how we *give* thanks to others but also about how we *receive* things in the world. It requires us to pay attention to the good things we get and to observe our own internal reactions to them. Indeed, children who learn to deeply receive things in their lives may have the most genuine experiences of gratitude. These experiences, in turn, may motivate them to spontaneously engage in behaviors of thanks and appreciation.

Our understanding of gratitude's development is, of course, incomplete. More work needs to be done to identify other potential precursors to gratitude, the stages that children progress through, and how gratitude develops over time in the brain, as well as how this process varies across cultures. There are some indicators, however, that once children near adulthood, gratitude may start to take on new meaning—not just as a social custom or a form of reciprocity but as a deep moral value, one that has the power to profoundly move us.

CHAPTER 4

What Can the Brain Reveal About Gratitude?

By Glenn Fox

When I first embarked on the journey to study gratitude, I came across philosophical treatises and religious exhortations emphasizing the importance of gratitude, along with scientific studies suggesting that gratitude can improve your sleep, enhance your romantic relationships, protect you from illness, motivate you to exercise, and boost your happiness, among many other benefits. At the time, however, very little was known about what happens in our brains and bodies when we experience gratitude.

As a neuroscientist, I zeroed in on the neurobiology of gratitude with a specific question in mind: can our brain activity reveal anything about how gratitude achieves its significant benefits? Given the clear relationship between mental and physical health, understanding what happens in the brain when we feel gratitude could tell us more about the mind-body connection—namely, how feeling positive emotion can improve bodily functions. These results could benefit scientists designing programs to generate gratitude by helping them focus on the precise activities and experiences most essential to reaping gratitude's benefits.

How to Make a Brain Grateful

It must be said that actually capturing people in the moment of feeling gratitude posed some challenges. After all, some people may not feel gratitude when we expect them to, and others may even feel grateful in unexpected situations. My best bet would be to try to induce gratitude through powerful stories of aid and sacrifice.

The USC Shoah Foundation Institute for Visual History houses the world's largest repository of videotaped Holocaust survivor testimonies—many of which are filled with breathtaking acts of selflessness and generosity. My team of undergraduates and I watched hundreds of hours of survivor testimony, honing in on stories in which the survivor received help of some kind from another person. We then transformed a collection of these stories into short scenarios that we shared with our study's participants.

Each scenario was rephrased into the second person ("You are on a wintertime death march and a fellow prisoner gives you a warm coat"). We asked study participants to imagine themselves in the scenario and, as much as possible, how they would feel if they were in the same situation. While participants reflected on the gift and the feeling of receiving it, we measured their brain activity using modern brain imaging techniques, in the form of functional magnetic resonance imaging (fMRI).

Finally, for each of these scenarios, we asked participants how much gratitude they felt as they imagined this gift, and we correlated this rating with their brain activity in that moment. While imagination will not elicit exactly the same feelings as actually living through such situations, participants overwhelmingly reported deep engagement in the task and strong feelings of gratitude for the kindness and selflessness they imagined witnessing or experiencing.

What's more, our results revealed that when participants reported those grateful feelings, their brains showed activity in a set of regions located in the medial prefrontal cortex, an area in the frontal lobes of the brain where the two hemispheres meet. This area of the brain is associated with understanding other people's perspectives, empathy, and feelings of relief. This is also an area of the brain that is massively connected to the systems in the body and brain that regulate emotion and support the process of stress relief.

More Reasons to Be Grateful

These data told us a reasonable story about gratitude. The regions associated with gratitude are part of the neural networks that light up when we socialize and experience pleasure. These regions are also heavily connected to the parts of the brain that control basic emotion regulation, such as heart rate and arousal levels, and are associated with stress relief and thus pain reduction. They are also closely linked to the brain's *mu opioid* networks, which are activated during close interpersonal touch and relief from pain—these networks may have evolved in early humans out of the need for grooming one another for parasites.

In other words, our data suggest that gratitude's reliance on the brain networks associated with social bonding and stress relief may explain in part how grateful feelings lead to health benefits over time. Feeling grateful and recognizing help from others creates a more relaxed body state and allows the subsequent benefits of lowered stress to wash over us.

Perhaps even more encouraging, researcher Prathik Kini and colleagues at Indiana University performed a subsequent study examining how practicing gratitude can alter brain function in depressed individuals. They found evidence that gratitude may induce structural changes in the same parts of the brain that we found active in our experiment. Such a result, in complement to our own, tells a story of how the mental practice of gratitude may even be able to change and rewire the brain.

Of course, these findings are only the first steps in a much longer process. My colleagues and I are heartened by the growth of gratitude research and encourage other research groups to join us in studying this powerful emotion. What is clear so far is the deep and serious need to continue studying gratitude and exploring its capacities.

CHAPTER 5

The Surprising Neural Link Between Giving and Gratitude

By Christina Karns

As Glenn Fox showed in the previous chapter, gratitude activates parts of the brain associated with socializing and experiencing pleasure. My own work has zeroed in on one dimension of that association—between gratitude and our willingness to help someone else. I am discovering that the neural connection between the two is very deep and that cultivating gratitude may encourage us to feel more generous. We don't offer thanks for selfish reasons. Far from it: gratitude, like giving, might be its own reward.

In research on the relationship between gratitude and altruism—the intent to help someone else, even if it's at a cost to ourselves—there are generally two approaches. One is to conduct a survey; the other is to conduct an experiment.

First, we can ask whether people who seem to be more grateful are also more altruistic. Researchers use questionnaires to determine the degree to which someone is characteristically grateful, and they ask other questions to determine the degree to which someone is generally giving. Finally, they use statistics to determine the extent to which someone's altruism could be predicted from their gratitude. Such studies are helpful for understanding the way gratitude could relate to altruism—in fact, the two do appear to go hand in hand—but of course, they depend on a person's ability to judge their own gratitude and altruism. We can imagine someone touting themselves as tremendously grateful, or the most generous person since Mother Teresa, but this could certainly be untrue. That's why studies using these methods cannot explain why grateful people might behave prosocially; they can only indicate that they do. Perhaps they just feel guilty. Or perhaps altruistic people feel good when other people do well. How can we know?

The experimental approach could prove helpful here. In one recent study, some colleagues of mine tried to understand the relationship between general prosocial tendencies and the way the brain responds to charitable donations. To start, the researchers assessed the prosocial tendencies of the participants using questionnaires. Then they supplied participants with real money and put them in an MRI scanner that measures blood-oxygen levels in the brain. The money could go to either the participants themselves or a charity, such as a local food bank. As the money transferred, my colleagues focused on activity in the reward centers of the brain—the regions that give us a dose of feel-good neurotransmitters—to compare the brain's response to the conditions.

The result? My colleagues found that the more prosocial partici-pants felt far more inner reward when the money went to charity than when it went to themselves. They found something else interesting: the older the participant, the larger this benevolent disposition—suggest-ing that, with age, your brain may reward you more when you see good in the world rather than when you get some personal benefit.

This study answered some big questions but also left others unan-swered. One of these unanswered questions involved the link between gratitude and altruism. Do they go hand in hand? Does gratitude actu-ally encourage altruism? Stepping back from results like these, we're also left to wonder about what makes someone grateful or altruistic in the first place. Is it a matter of the right dose of prosocial genes? Or is it a lifetime of experiences or family socialization that encourages both gratitude and giving? These are questions raised throughout this book, because scientists are still searching for the answers.

To start to find out, my own team conducted another experiment that was quite similar to the one just described. The key difference? We asked participants about their gratitude levels as well as their altruism, with a simpler version of the giving task. After they performed their giving activity in the MRI machines, we compared the brain's response for outcomes that benefited charity versus self, just as in the previous study. We found that the participants who reported more grateful and more altruistic traits had a stronger response in the reward regions of the brain when the money went to charity than when it went to themselves, just as in the previous study. We were excited to find this result in a new group of people with a similar, but not identical, task.

There were significant differences between our study and the earlier one. Our study included only young women. While the earlier study had shown the neural and behavioral measure of benevolence increasing with age, no one had yet shown that this measure could change over a shorter time span in healthy young adults. This led to another big question that needed to be answered: could gratitude practice lead to more altruistic tendencies in the brain?

In step two of the experiment, we randomly assigned half of the participants to write a gratitude journal entry every evening until another brain scan three weeks later. The other half of the group wrote expressive journal entries, but the prompts for these entries were neutral rather than gratitude focused. Neither group was told what the purpose of the study was or what other people were doing. At the end of three weeks, participants came back for their second brain scan. Once again, the key measurement was the brain's reward response to where the money went—a charity or themselves. Would the reward response change more with the gratitude group than with the control group? Indeed, it did! The response in the ventromedial prefrontal cortex, a key region for reward processing in the brain, showed an increase in the pure altruism measure for the gratitude group and a decrease in the control group.

Of course, many factors can influence the brain's reward processing. We can imagine that receiving $5 could feel great...or it could make you feel cheated if you were expecting more. It really depends. However, we found that after our study's participants practiced gratitude for three weeks, the ventromedial prefrontal cortex increased the value it placed on benefits to others. And this was for tax-like transfers, when participants didn't even get to congratulate themselves on making an altruistic choice. The computer did the choosing for them; they just observed the result. They lost five bucks, but the charity gained it—and their brains felt better about the outcome.

In a sense, gratitude seems to prepare the brain for generosity. Counting blessings is quite different from counting your cash, because gratitude, just as philosophers and psychologists predict, points us toward moral behaviors, reciprocity, and pay-it-forward motivations. Apparently, our brain literally makes us feel richer when others do well. Perhaps this is why researchers have observed that grateful people give more.

Gratitude might be good for us—but it is good for others as well.

How Gratitude Relates to Other Emotions

By Summer Allen

In this chapter, neuroscientist Christina Karns describes how feelings of gratitude and generosity go together in our brains. Hers isn't the only study to examine how gratitude relates to other emotions.

Some researchers have looked at gratitude and the condition of owing someone, known as *indebtedness*. While it seems like feelings of gratitude and indebtedness might overlap, they can be experimentally separated. For example, studies have found that people feel significantly more grateful when they know a helper has benevolent intentions than when they suspect a favor is given with ulterior motives, and a recipient's gratitude decreases and indebtedness increases when their benefactor expresses a greater expectation of repayment. Additionally, more self-focused people tend to experience more indebtedness and less gratitude.

Other studies have attempted to distinguish gratitude from other positive emotions, such as *elevation*, the emotion that we feel when witnessing moral actions. Work by Sara Algoe and Jonathan Haidt, for example, suggests that the three "other-praising emotions"—elevation, gratitude, and admiration—can be separated based on the outcomes that these emotions motivate: "Elevation (a response to moral excellence) motivates prosocial and affiliative behavior, gratitude motivates improved relationships with benefactors, and admiration motivates self-improvement."

Gratitude is also often conflated with appreciation. One study defines appreciation as "acknowledging the value and meaning of something—an event, a person, a behavior, an object—and feeling a positive emotional connection to it" and treats gratitude as one of eight key facets of appreciation: "The gratitude aspect of appreciation refers to noticing and acknowledging a benefit that has been received, whether from another person or deity, and feeling thankful for the efforts, sacrifices, and actions of an 'other.'"

Another study found that appreciation "made a significant unique contribution to life satisfaction" after controlling for both other personality factors and trait gratitude—a result that suggests appreciation may be worthy of further consideration in its own right, independent of gratitude. However, yet another study found that people's levels of appreciation and their dispositional gratitude levels are highly correlated with one another; this result suggests that appreciation and gratitude may be too interrelated to be considered separate traits. Thus, the scientific distinctions between appreciation and gratitude are still a matter of debate and discussion.

PART 2

The Impact of Gratitude

In this part, researchers and journalists describe some of the most significant and recent studies on the social, physical, and psychological benefits of gratitude. They also touch on some of gratitude's trickier aspects. While the benefits tend to be straightforward, as you will hear in the first essay, "Why Gratitude Is Good for Us," gratitude can also trigger negative feelings.

For example, gratitude might trigger anxiety in men because they fear it makes them feel weak, to their detriment. In "How Cultural Differences Shape Gratitude and Its Impact," Kira Newman highlights how thankfulness sometimes gets lost in translation—and can even land with a thud.

In the end, as Eric Pedersen and Debra Lieberman argue, gratitude in all its forms is an essential tool for building cooperation. The question—to be explored in the pages to come—is how to learn to express our feelings in ways that will strengthen our relationships.

CHAPTER 6

Why Gratitude Is Good for Us

By Joel Wong, Joshua Brown, Christina Armenta,
Sonja Lyubomirsky, Summer Allen,
Amie Gordon, and Kira Newman

What impact does gratitude have on our lives? Is it beneficial to our brains and bodies? Are there any negative effects?

The first part of this book introduced some of the methods scientists have used to understand the roots of gratitude in our brains and bodies. To study its effects on people, scientists have either observed people who are already grateful or conducted experiments to help people cultivate gratitude. For example, in some studies, participants were induced to feel thankful with a small gift of money or a little unexpected help. Other studies have asked people to remember moments when they felt grateful, write letters of gratitude to important others, or keep gratitude journals (where they listed things in their lives for which they are thankful). The best experiments also include a control group of people as a comparison, who haven't received a gift or done a gratitude practice, but sometimes engage in other activities (like keeping journals about their days).

What have scientists found so far? Across two decades of research, gratitude in its various forms seems to have wide-ranging benefits for our mental health, our relationships, our physical health, and our self-improvement. And ultimately, gratitude makes us not just feel good but also *do* good, sharing its advantages with the people around us.

Gratitude Makes Us Feel Good

Gratitude is, in part, a positive emotion, so it should come as no surprise that being grateful tends to bring us greater well-being.

In research by Robert Emmons, Sonja Lyubomirsky, and many other scientists, practicing gratitude has proven to be one of the most reliable methods for increasing happiness and life satisfaction; it also boosts feelings of optimism, joy, pleasure, enthusiasm, and other positive emotions.

In one study testing different activities to boost happiness, researchers compared writing and delivering a gratitude letter in person to activities focused exclusively on the self, like identifying or using your personal strengths. In the end, the gratitude group experienced the most benefits out of all the participants. They reported feeling happier and less depressed after expressing their gratitude and continued to be so for a full month.

It's so easy to get used to the good things in our lives that we really need to put effort into appreciating them, even when they're little things. Gratitude helps us savor our positive experiences and prevents us from taking things for granted. And tasks like the gratitude journal are an easy way to encourage the regular practice of gratitude.

Other studies suggest that practicing gratitude can be helpful for people who are struggling in life. Two contributors to this chapter—Joel Wong and Joshua Brown—studied nearly three hundred adults, mostly college students who were seeking mental health counseling. Before the participants began counseling, researchers randomly assigned them into three groups. Although all three groups received counseling services, the first group was also instructed to write a letter of gratitude to another person each week for three weeks, whereas the second group was asked to write about their deepest thoughts and feelings about negative experiences. The third group did not do any writing activity.

What did Wong, Brown, and their colleagues find? Those who wrote gratitude letters reported significantly better mental health four weeks and twelve weeks after their writing exercise ended, compared with the others. Participants were more satisfied with their lives, experiencing fewer symptoms of anxiety and depression, and they were able to function better in their relationships and life overall. This suggests that gratitude writing can be beneficial not just for healthy, well-adjusted individuals but also for those who struggle with mental health concerns. In fact, it seems, practicing gratitude on top of receiving psychological counseling carries greater benefits than having counseling alone, even when that gratitude practice is brief. Other studies support the notion that gratitude could be a helpful part of therapy and may reduce depression among people with chronic disease.

But why would counting your blessings be helpful when life seems dark? According to an analysis of the gratitude letters, gratitude may work by unshackling us from toxic emotions. Wong and Brown compared the percentage of positive emotion words, negative emotion words, and *we* words (first-person plural words) that participants used in their writing. Not surprisingly, those in the gratitude group used a higher percentage of positive emotion words and *we* words, and a lower percentage of negative emotion words, than those in the other writing group. However, it wasn't the use of more positive emotion words and more *we* words that corresponded to better mental health; it was only when people used fewer negative emotion words that they saw mental health benefits. Perhaps this suggests that writing gratitude letters produces better mental health by shifting our attention away from toxic emotions, such as resentment and envy. When you write about how grateful you are to others and how much other people have blessed your life, it might become considerably harder for you to ruminate on your negative experiences.

Gratitude Improves Our Relationships

Gratitude is not a solo experience, of course. When we practice gratitude, we are often grateful for someone in particular, reflecting on their lovable quirks or the beautiful bond we have with them. And that experience can lead us to feel closer and more connected to the people around us.

In another study, two contributors to this chapter—Christina Armenta and Sonja Lyubomirsky—asked adults and college students in the United States and Korea to perform two different gratitude activities: either recalling a grateful experience or writing a letter of gratitude. Compared to other pleasant activities—like hiking or shopping—gratitude in particular seemed to generate positive social feelings. Participants felt more connected to others and more elevated—moved, uplifted, and optimistic about humanity. In another study, Armenta and Lyubomirsky found similar benefits among ninth- and tenth-grade students who wrote gratitude letters.

Gratitude not only seems to help us deepen ties with others but also may make us more satisfied with our existing relationships. Another contributor to this chapter, Amie Gordon, and her colleagues published a series of studies that found thankfulness can help intimate relationships thrive by promoting a cycle of generosity. That is, one partner's gratitude can prompt both partners to think and act in ways that convey gratitude to each other and promote commitment to their relationship. Here's how it works.

Step 1. Couples Who Feel More Grateful Want to Hold on to Their Relationship

This part of the process is very simple: moments of gratitude help people recognize the value in their partners—and a valuable partner is worth holding on to, of course. The researchers found this to be true in a number of studies. When people feel more appreciative than usual of their partners, they also say they feel more committed.

And this benefit of gratitude has long-term consequences. The more grateful people were at the beginning of the study, the more committed they were nine months later. So, it seems that grateful partners are more motivated to maintain a relationship.

Step 2. Couples Who Feel More Grateful Work to Keep Their Relationship

Being motivated to stay in a relationship is only part of the story. We also need to act on that motivation. And gratitude is valuable here as well: experiencing gratitude also seems to promote behaviors that help people hold on to their relationships.

In one study, Gordon and colleagues found that people reported being more thoughtful and responsive to their partners' needs on days when they felt more grateful for their partners. In another study, the researchers brought couples into the lab and had them talk about important topics in their relationships. Participants who were more grateful for their partners were observed as being more caring and attentive listeners during these discussions—a key for promoting intimacy. Other research finds that feeling grateful toward others—even strangers!—makes us want to spend more time with them.

These findings suggest that gratitude might help people gain and maintain intimacy with each other.

Step 3. Working to Keep the Relationship Makes the Other Partner Feel Appreciated

This is where the good stuff happens. Recognizing you have a valuable partner and acting accordingly can help your partner feel more valued.

In a lab study of couples, Gordon and colleagues found that participants who were better listeners during those conversations in the lab—meaning, for instance, they asked clarifying questions—had partners who reported feeling more appreciated by them.

Step 4. When a Partner Feels Appreciated, They Are More Grateful

Now we complete the cycle. In this research, we find that an appreciated partner is a grateful partner. On days when people report feeling more appreciated by their partner, their own feelings of gratitude for their partner increase. And this makes sense: what partner is more valuable than someone who clearly values you?

And this is where the benefits of gratitude really take off. Going back to the initial steps in this cycle, we remember that grateful partners are those who will think and act in ways that help them hold on to their relationships. So now, both partners are focused on maintaining the relationship. In this way, that first moment of gratitude has the power to spark an ongoing cycle of gratitude and generosity (until one of you is too tired, stressed, or anxious). One study on gratitude in couples does highlight a potential barrier to this cycle of gratitude and generosity: more grateful people who have less grateful partners become less satisfied with their relationships over time. In this way, it takes both partners' engaging in gratitude and generosity to create and maintain such a cycle.

Over time, this helps explain why gratitude leads to more committed and longer-lasting romantic relationships. And a similar dynamic may operate in other types of relationships, too—with friends, at work, in the neighborhood.

Keep in mind that gratitude in relationships isn't just about saying thanks after your partner takes out the trash. Gratitude includes appreciating not only what someone does but also who they are as a person. You're not just thankful that your partner took out the trash but thankful that you have a partner who is thoughtful enough to know that you hate taking out the trash. Gratitude means thinking about people's best traits and remembering why you formed a connection with them in the first place. Being grateful may help you see all the love and support you have around you.

Gratitude Benefits Our Health

The benefits of gratitude aren't confined to our minds. Mental and physical health are intertwined, and there is increasing evidence that gratitude leaves a stamp on our physical bodies. This shows up in ways you might even notice on a day-to-day basis. In one study, more grateful participants reported fewer health problems (such as headaches, gastrointestinal problems, respiratory infections, and sleep disturbances); in another, more grateful participants reported fewer physical symptoms (including headaches, dizziness, stomachaches, and runny noses). People of all ages and various nationalities who have more grateful dispositions have fewer health complaints than their less grateful counterparts.

Even if you're not naturally grateful, practicing gratitude could also alleviate your aches and pains. In a 2003 study by Robert Emmons and Michael McCullough, three groups of college students wrote just once a week for ten weeks about things they were grateful for, neutral life events, or hassles. Over the course of the experiment, the gratitude group reported fewer physical symptoms (such as headaches, shortness of breath, sore muscles, and nausea) than the others.

Beyond these outward symptoms, under the skin, gratitude may affect biological processes that support health. Inflammation is an immune response that can have negative effects on the body, including the cardiovascular system. According to one study, gratitude journaling for eight weeks can reduce markers of inflammation, at least for patients with a certain type of heart failure. More grateful people also have significantly lower levels of a protein found in red blood cells called hemoglobin A1c (HbA1c), which is associated with risk of heart failure and heart attacks, diabetes, chronic kidney disease, various cancers, and death.

The heartwarming power of gratitude may even extend to our actual hearts. In 1995, a study found that people feeling appreciation (an emotion related to gratitude) have improved heart rate variability, an indicator of good heart health. In a study from 2016, women who kept a gratitude journal where they wrote about "previously unappreciated people and things in their lives" for two weeks ended up with lower blood pressure than those who wrote about daily events.

And being grateful may help patients recover from a heart attack. In a study by Jeff Huffman and his colleagues, more optimistic and more grateful people showed signs of improved blood vessel function two weeks—though not six months—after being hospitalized for heart attacks, compared to less grateful patients. (Note that this finding is for *trait* gratitude—how inclined participants already were to be grateful people. Studies of the impact of gratitude exercises get somewhat different results.)

The way gratitude shows up in the brain may underlie some of its health benefits. As you saw in part 1, gratitude relies on the brain networks associated with social bonding and stress relief. Feeling grateful and recognizing help from others may create a more relaxed body state and allow the subsequent benefits of lowered stress to wash over us.

On the level of behavior, gratitude may also promote day-to-day activities that keep us healthy, like sleep and physical exercise. Sleep, of course, is vital for good health. Inadequate sleep puts strain on the body and increases our risk of developing obesity, diabetes, cardiovascular disease, and other conditions. But anyone who has struggled with insomnia knows it's not always so easy to catch enough z's. Well, those of us counting sheep may want to try counting blessings instead. In a study of 401 people—40 percent of whom had clinically impaired sleep—more grateful people reported falling asleep more quickly, sleeping longer, having better sleep quality, and staying awake more easily during the day. This study also found evidence that more grateful people sleep better because they have fewer negative thoughts and more positive ones at bedtime—less lying awake rehearsing fights with loved ones or stressing about money. People with chronic pain and heart failure who are more grateful report sleeping better, despite their condition, than less grateful patients.

You don't have to be a natural gratitude guru to get good sleep; evidence suggests that just performing brief, simple gratitude exercises can help. In Emmons and McCullough's 2003 study, mentioned previously, people with neuromuscular disease who kept a daily gratitude journal for three weeks reported sleeping longer at night and feeling more refreshed than people who journaled about other things. And in the 2016 study of women keeping a gratitude journal for two weeks, the women reported slightly better sleep quality compared to women who performed other tasks.

Besides aiding slumber, gratitude may lead people to engage in other behaviors that help keep them healthy, like eating well and not smoking. Indeed, more grateful people report having healthier lifestyles. They adopt better nutrition and exercise habits, and they're more likely to see a doctor for their health concerns. College students who count blessings weekly for ten weeks also exercise more than those who do other writing activities, and more grateful adolescents engage in less substance use and risky sexual behaviors. When researchers followed patients who had survived a heart attack, the survivors who were more optimistic and grateful two weeks later were also most likely to follow their doctors' recommendations half a year later.

So, gratitude seems to affect our health on three levels: how we feel on a daily basis, what's going on in our bodies, and what kind of behaviors we engage in. Of course, these aspects of health are interdependent, and it's too soon to tell where gratitude exerts its strongest influence. Some of these benefits may result from the health-enhancing positive emotions and relationships that gratitude nurtures, while others may be more direct. For now, the research suggests that having a grateful disposition or working on your gratitude muscles may be part of an overall healthy lifestyle.

Gratitude Helps Us Do Good

Christina Armenta, Sonja Lyubomirsky, and their team have found that gratitude is an activating, energizing force that may lead us to pursue our goals and become better, more socially engaged people. According to this work, gratitude and kindness are inextricably intertwined. Gratitude is more than just a common response to kindness, because it inspires us to perform kind acts for others—whether as a form of thanks or to pay it forward to someone else. For example, in a 2006 study, researchers Monica Bartlett and David DeSteno figured out an ingenious way to engineer feelings of gratitude and related acts of kindness. Participants were filling out surveys on computers in groups of two, when one participant's computer suddenly went blank. In fact, the other participant (a confederate who was secretly working with the researchers) had covertly pulled the plug on the first participant's monitor. The real participant was told that a technician was on the way, and they might have to start their task over—but the confederate swooped in and, after some nosing around, "discovered" the loose plug, so the other participant could continue their task.

After receiving this help and feeling grateful, people were more willing to help their benefactors—even though that help took the form of filling out a tedious survey—compared to people who were either induced to feel amused or not induced to feel any emotion at all. Interestingly, people who felt grateful were also more likely to help complete strangers! Gratitude, therefore, not only improves our own lot in life but motivates us to improve the circumstances of those around us.

Once again, something seems to be going on at the level of the brain during this process. In their study of three hundred college students mentioned earlier in the chapter, Joel Wong, Joshua Brown, and their team brought participants back into the lab after three months for an fMRI scan. While researchers measured brain activity, participants performed a pay-it-forward task. They were given a small amount of money by a nice person, who only asked that they pass the money on to someone if they felt grateful.

Participants then decided how much of the money, if any, to pass on to a worthy cause (which was, in fact, donated to a local charity). Researchers also gave them questionnaires to measure how grateful they were in their lives in general.

Ultimately, Wong and colleagues found that when people who were generally more grateful gave more money to a cause, they showed greater neural sensitivity in the medial prefrontal cortex, the same area that activates when people are feeling gratitude. Furthermore, those assigned to write gratitude letters showed greater sensitivity in the medial prefrontal cortex when expressing gratitude, even three months after the letter writing. In a related study led by Christina Karns—described by her in chapter 5—practicing gratitude for three weeks led to a stronger response in the reward regions of the brain when watching money get transferred to charity.

Grateful brains, then, seem to place more value on benefits to others. With this in mind, we can see kindness and generously paying it forward as neurologically linked with the experience of gratitude.

In addition to inspiring us to improve the lives of others, gratitude may also spur us to take initiative to improve our own lives. Indeed, gratitude has been linked with success and achievement in multiple life domains, including work and academics. For instance, a 2011 study by Robert Emmons and Anjali Mishra found that people feel motivated and energized when they experience gratitude, and that gratitude encourages them to make progress toward their goals. In this study, students were instructed to list the goals they wanted to accomplish within the next two months and were then randomly assigned to count their blessings, list their hassles, or complete a neutral writing activity each week for ten weeks. Those in the gratitude group reported making relatively more progress toward their goals. In addition, a 2009 study led by Nathaniel Lambert suggests that gratitude leads people to believe they deserve positive outcomes and are capable of achieving them.

As for young people, grateful students tend to have higher GPAs, participate in more extracurricular activities, and have a stronger desire to contribute to society. And those previously mentioned grateful ninth and tenth graders—who thanked parents, teachers, or coaches—increased their desire to improve themselves as well as their confidence and competence in working toward this self-improvement.

Together, these findings suggest that gratitude is a motivating emotion that spurs people to action. However, little research has directly explored precisely how gratitude might motivate us. Why does gratitude inspire positive action rather than, say, breeding complacency or having no effect at all?

Armenta, Lyubomirsky, and colleagues identified several pathways through which expressing gratitude can motivate people to improve themselves and their communities.

Social Pathways

First, the kind of deep and supportive relationships that gratitude promotes can also motivate and sustain our efforts at self-improvement. Why might this be the case? Think about it this way: by strengthening our social bonds, gratitude rewards us with a strong network of support and encouragement, thus leading us to feel that we are capable of tackling big challenges. For example, a woman may feel grateful to a friend who helped her recover from an illness. This may make her feel closer and more connected to her friend as well as prompt her to eat healthier and exercise more, to prove to her friend that the time her friend spent helping her get better was not wasted. This feeling of connectedness may also remind the woman that people care about her and want her to be healthy.

Feeling close and connected to others may motivate us to improve ourselves and become better people because we want to prove that we are worthy of our relationships and because we feel encouraged, supported, and inspired by the people in our lives.

Elevation

Elevation, again, is scientists' name for the uplifting feeling we get when we see people performing great acts of kindness; it is associated with a warmth in the chest and feeling moved to be a better person. Importantly, feeling elevated inspires people to be more generous, perhaps to emulate the moral acts of others.

Armenta and Lyubomirsky believe that gratitude makes people feel elevated—which then bolsters their motivation and effort toward self-improvement. Notably, they found evidence for this idea among both undergraduates and working adults. In one six-week study, the researchers prompted undergraduates either to write a letter of gratitude to someone who did something kind for them or to list their daily activities each week. All of the students were then instructed to do acts of kindness for others as a self-improvement activity. Students who expressed gratitude reported feeling more elevated—and, in turn, they exerted more effort on their kind acts toward others. Therefore, elevation may be one way that expressing gratitude can motivate students to try harder to be better, kinder people.

In a similar four-week study, the researchers prompted corporate employees to write weekly gratitude letters to someone who had helped them with their work, their health, or something else. These employees were then encouraged to try to improve themselves by becoming kinder, excelling at work, or improving their health. Employees in another group were instructed only to list their daily activities each week and focus on general self-improvement. All employees had the freedom to choose which steps they took to improve themselves.

Relative to employees who only listed their daily activities each week, employees who wrote gratitude letters felt more moved, uplifted, and inspired to be better people, which then increased their productivity at work and boosted their sense of autonomy at the end of the study. These findings suggest that elevation—that is, feeling inspired and uplifted—may motivate us to become better, more productive workers as well as healthier and more generous people.

Humility

Armenta and Lyubomirsky believe that gratitude spurs us to become more humble, because expressing gratitude takes the focus off of ourselves and forces us to recognize that our successes are due, at least in part, to the actions of other people. Sure enough, their lab has found evidence that gratitude promotes more frequent humble feelings. Furthermore, in a 2014 study led by their colleague Elliott Kruse, participants were randomly assigned either to write a letter of gratitude or to write about what they did during the previous two hours. All participants then had to imagine someone was angry with them and describe their reaction to that person. Those in the gratitude group wrote more humble responses—for example, they were more inclined to consider the other person's point of view and were more likely to accept blame.

Because humility enables us to see clearly how others have supported us, it may encourage us to engage in positive behaviors, such as helping others and bettering ourselves, to pay back the people who have helped us along the way. For example, a student may feel humbled by all the time his math teacher spent encouraging him and making sure he understood how to solve math problems. This feeling of humility may motivate him to want to do better in school—by taking advantage of tutoring services or engaging in extracurricular activities—to prove to himself and to his teacher that the time and energy spent on him was not misplaced.

Taken together, then, the evidence strongly suggests that gratitude doesn't lead us to relax, stagnate, and become complacent. Instead, it often motivates us to become better people. It looks like gratitude inspires us to put forth more effort toward school, work, our communities, and our relationships, perhaps even prompting us to strive for goals we would otherwise not have thought possible.

The Promise of Gratitude

The promise of gratitude is not just to make us happy and healthy but also to motivate us to improve our own lives—and even, one might say, become more productive members of society and better citizens of the world. Of course, talking about gratitude in general is too simplistic. Some of its benefits are enjoyed by naturally grateful people, while others seem to come from keeping a journal or writing a gratitude letter. It sometimes takes weeks of practice before those benefits appear, and we don't always know how long they'll last. They might even depend on how often you practice—like whether you journal every week or every few days.

Still, gratitude is one of the most scientifically backed practices in positive psychology. It may not be able to solve every personal problem, but we do know that it orients our brains toward the positive and the social: those nourishing resources that already exist around us. We know that it helps combat the brain's tendency to focus on the negative and get used to good things. And it might just change the lens through which we see the world, transforming our health and well-being in the process.

How Gratitude Can Help You Achieve Your Goals

By David DeSteno

In my research, I've found gratitude to be very helpful for self-control. For example, we asked people to recall a time when they felt grateful, happy, or neutral. We then asked them to make several choices of the form, "Would you rather have $X now or $Y in Z days?"—where Y was always greater than X, and the number of Z days varied. We found that feeling grateful almost doubled people's self-control—the grateful participants were more willing to wait for the future reward than those who were feeling happy or neutral. These findings mirror a more recent study showing a connection between levels of daily gratitude and greater average patience and self-control.

Gratitude's benefits for self-control also extend to being willing to sacrifice to help others. In one experiment, for example, we made some people feel grateful by having an actor come to their aid in solving a problem we had rigged in the lab. After leaving the lab, participants were asked to help out another person with a project that involved doing hard problems. Those who had experienced gratitude volunteered to persevere with the problems longer, even though they were not being watched or in any way compelled, and even though they may have had to stay longer in order to do so.

Gratitude leads to perseverance in other contexts, as well. For example, researcher Alice Isen found that doctors who were nudged toward feeling grateful were more willing to spend the time necessary for a proper reading of a patient file, which led to more accurate diagnoses. All of this research shows that gratitude helps people be more future-oriented and exhibit more self-control. And, unlike willpower, gratitude doesn't require much effort—people seem to enjoy expressing it.

If you have problems being grateful—if you feel that your own hard work was responsible for any success you've experienced—try recalling events that were integral to reaching your goals. Maybe you had good mentoring early in your school or work career, or someone helped you financially, or you happened to be in the right place at the right time. Even luck, when reframed in this way, can lead to a feeling of gratitude.

Can Gratitude Fix Everything?

By Kira Newman

Despite the great variety of benefits that gratitude seems to have, it is not a panacea. In fact, a handful of studies have failed to find certain benefits to a gratitude practice.

In the study by Huffman and colleagues where they tested gratitude in patients who had had heart attacks, gratitude didn't seem to increase the patients' physical activity or decrease their likelihood of being readmitted to the hospital over time.

Other studies have found that shorter-term practices of gratitude may not be enough to have a positive impact. In one study of middle school students, those who completed a "counting blessings" activity for two weeks didn't report better physical health than other groups. And, in their 2003 study, Emmons and McCullough found that college students who kept daily gratitude journals for two weeks didn't fare better in terms of health complaints. Emmons and McCullough also found that people with neuromuscular disease who kept a daily gratitude journal for three weeks reported the same amount of physical pain as people who didn't.

Do these mixed results mean that keeping a gratitude journal or writing gratitude letters won't improve your health or lead to other benefits? Not necessarily. Future studies will need to test this possibility. When it comes to gratitude journaling, for instance, it could be that people who keep a gratitude journal for longer—say, multiple months—see stronger effects. And the length of your practice is just one factor upon which the success of gratitude may depend—alongside which type of practice you do, whom you tend to direct your gratitude toward, or some of your individual traits (like age, gender, religion, or personality). There is a lot we still don't yet know about the effects of gratitude on our bodies, minds, relationships, and communities.

CHAPTER 7

How Gender Shapes Gratitude
By Summer Allen

When it comes to gratitude, does gender make a difference? Are women socialized to feel gratitude differently from men? Do men feel less thankful, and does that give them an advantage over women? Or is gratitude a strength for women?

The research to date suggests that women do tend to feel more grateful than men—and that this isn't necessarily to their detriment. While a surfeit of gratitude may sometimes have negative consequences for women, a gratitude deficit may have worse repercussions for men. Of course, we all likely know super grateful men and unthankful women; gender differences in gratitude are sometimes overblown. But research suggests that men, on average, are less grateful than women. For example, a 2012 survey of two thousand Americans, commissioned by the John Templeton Foundation, found evidence of a gratitude gender gap: "Women are more likely than men to express gratitude on a regular basis (52 percent women/44 percent men), feel that they have much in life to be thankful [for] (64 percent women/50 percent men), and express gratitude to a wider variety of people."

Studies of middle school and high school students, undergraduates, and older adults have found that women report feeling slightly more grateful than men in their day-to-day lives—that is, they're more likely to feel trait, or dispositional, gratitude. Studies have also found that women are more likely than men to report feeling grateful to God. Importantly, there is also some evidence that men, on average, are less likely to express gratitude, too.

So, it appears from the research that the average man may be slightly less grateful—or report feeling less grateful—than the average woman. But is this difference meaningful?

"The effect is small, but just because it's small doesn't mean it's not meaningful," says Todd Kashdan, professor of psychology and director of the Laboratory for the Study of Social Anxiety, Character Strengths, and Related Phenomena at George Mason University. Kashdan notes that the gender difference is larger for expressing gratitude than experiencing it—and the effect is bigger for older men than younger ones. "Based on baby boomers, we know that there's a particular psychological profile of being a little bit more rigid, masculine," he says. "They encapsulate the essence of masculinity with all of its good sides and bad sides. This is one of the bad sides."

There is limited evidence that this gratitude gender disparity may be particularly bad for American men—at least compared to German men. A 1988 study comparing the experience of emotions in men and women of different ages from the United States and Germany found that German men reported experiencing gratitude significantly more often than American men did, and they viewed gratitude more positively—even "characterizing it as one of the most constructive emotions." American men, on the other hand, tended to report that gratitude was an undesirable and difficult-to-express emotion (even finding it humiliating in some cases). In fact, over a third of older men from the United States (aged thirty-five to fifty) said they would prefer to conceal gratitude than to openly express it.

Research suggests that there are downsides for men who struggle with gratitude. For starters, they're missing out on the well-known benefits of gratitude, such as increased happiness and life satisfaction. Philip Watkins's work, for example, has found that the relationship between gratitude and well-being is at least as strong for men as it is for women. Perhaps more importantly, men who have difficulties with gratitude in general—and especially in saying thanks aloud—may have a harder time building and maintaining relationships. This includes workplace relationships. "Gratitude is one of the easiest forms of social glue to create and maintain alliances in the workplace. It's simple. It's honest. It's genuine," says Kashdan. "So, if men are less likely to express their gratitude to other people, they are essentially shutting off a valve for forming alliances."

Why Do Some Men Struggle with Gratitude?

If gratitude is so important to success, why might some men have a harder time experiencing and expressing it? It turns out that receiving a gift, a favor, or help from someone else may be a more emotionally complicated experience for men, generally speaking. For example, Watkins says his work has found that the correlation between feeling gratitude and indebtedness—an obligation to repay a benefit—is about twice as high for men as it is for women (although the overall correlation between feeling gratitude and indebtedness is still quite low). And Kashdan and colleagues' 2009 study of gender differences in gratitude found that after receiving something of value or need, men reported feeling less gratitude and more obligation and burden than women reported feeling. Women, in general, reported feeling less uncertain and less conflicted by the experience. "Men are less willing to admit their dependence on others than women are," says Watkins. "We've argued that gratitude is heavier for men than it is for women."

Culture likely plays a role in this mixing of indebtedness and gratitude, especially for American men, as was proposed in the paper describing gratitude differences in American and German men. Perhaps because of the strong cultural expectations in the US that men be autonomous and fully self-sufficient, there may be a reluctance among men to express gratitude. To them, gratitude may signify a failure to act in a self-sufficient manner, and its expression might be taken to reflect dependency and weakness in relation to others.

Additionally, the culture of masculinity in the United States, which has tended to eschew vulnerability, may make experiencing— and expressing—gratitude difficult for some men. "The assumption has always been, 'Trust people and then you can be vulnerable,'" says

Kashdan. "And now the research is pretty clear that when you are vulnerable, this is what allows you to form and establish trust."

In fact, it may be impossible to be completely independent and invulnerable and still experience true gratitude. "Gratitude requires you to be vulnerable," says Kashdan. "You essentially have to acknowledge the fact that you cannot get through life without the benefits and the gifts and the strengths and the social resources and the intellectual resources of other people. You have to admit that you are not whole without other people."

There's another barrier to gratitude that applies to all genders. In a new study by Amit Kumar and Nicholas Epley of the University of Chicago, participants wrote gratitude letters to people who had touched their lives in a meaningful way. The researchers then asked the participants to predict how the recipient of their letter would feel after reading it, and then they asked the recipients how they actually felt. The result? The letter writers underestimated the positive impact of their letters and the surprise that the recipients felt about the content. They also overestimated how awkward the recipients would feel upon reading the letters.

And it makes sense: if you didn't feel your gratitude letter would have an impact, and if writing one feels like an act that would embarrass the person you're writing to, of course you wouldn't express your gratitude, especially in a gesture that seems so elaborate. "Wise decisions are guided by an accurate assessment of the expected value of action," Kumar and Epley write. "Underestimating the value of prosocial actions, such as expressing gratitude, may keep people from engaging in behavior that would maximize their own—and others'—well-being."

What Are the Best Ways to Get More Grateful?

The good news is that gratitude activities, such as keeping a gratitude journal or writing gratitude letters, can have serious benefits. Indeed, some research suggests that men—and boys—may have the most to gain by trying to increase the amount of gratitude they feel and express. For example, one study using gratitude journals found that only the male students became significantly more thankful by the end of a four-week experiment. In addition, those students felt more like they belonged at their school, which suggests that this type of activity could help students—particularly boys—feel more supported.

While the jury is still out as to whether gratitude activities definitively have better outcomes for men than women, a 2015 study by Watkins's group found that men who wrote down three things that made them feel grateful each day for a week became significantly happier compared to women assigned to the same activity. "We argued that women are already doing a lot of the kind of cognitive habits like counting your blessings might train you to do," says Watkins. "The interesting thing about that is that men enjoyed the exercises less than women, which is what we predicted, but they actually gained more from them."

If you are a person who has struggled with gratitude and is interested in becoming more grateful, there are a few evidence-based gratitude activities you could try, almost all of which are described throughout this book. These include gratitude journals, gratitude letters, gratitude meditations, savoring walks, and mental subtraction activities, where you appreciate someone by imagining your life without them.

Such an exercise might feel hard, at first, but displeasure may be a sign that you need to keep at it. "Sometimes our biggest barriers to happiness are there because they are things we need to overcome and may not be that enjoyable," Watkins says. "So, if you're not a very grateful person, like many men are not, to do a gratitude exercise is going to take more effort and you're not going to enjoy it as much at first, but that may be the very thing that you need to do to overcome that obstacle to happiness."

There may be other ways to work on gratitude skills that aren't gratitude exercises, per se. Kashdan points to acceptance and commitment therapy, which encourages people to figure out their values and create a schedule of behaviors that align with those values, as one method for increasing gratitude expression. "I think that the data are there; they're just not under the guise of gratitude right now," says Kashdan.

Another way to increase gratitude could be to try to address feelings of indebtedness that keep you from taking pleasure in feeling or expressing your gratitude, or at least try to make peace with feeling a mixture of indebtedness and gratitude. For instance, this could involve working on not seeing relationships as purely transactional: just because someone does something nice for you does not mean that you now owe them and need to immediately return the favor.

Luckily, there's a relatively simple way to reduce this feeling. Simply let people do nice things for you. Kashdan gives this example: "If somebody wants to pay your bill or buy you something, resist the temptation to say no." Instead, he says, "express your appreciation to them." When you do otherwise, "you've stolen positive experiences from both sides… and nobody feels good."

Equally important is to practice receiving other people's expressions of gratitude gracefully. "This is what people aren't talking about in the study and discussion of gratitude," says Kashdan. "I think people suck at this possibly more than being the giver of the gratitude expression." When someone thanks you, suggests Kashdan, "look them in the eye. Smile." Fight the urge to feel obligated to reciprocate; simply acknowledge their expression of gratitude, without dismissing it or minimizing whatever it is you did that they're thanking you for.

Kashdan knows what he's talking about, because receiving gratitude is something he's worked at. "I've gotten better at this only because I talk about this stuff regularly," he says. It's totally okay to "let them have their moment" of expressing gratitude and not scramble to express your own: "If you're intent to share your own compliment to match them, you've stolen the beauty of an expression of gratitude."

CHAPTER 8

How Cultural Differences Shape Gratitude and Its Impact

By Kira Newman

So far, this book has talked about gratitude in universal terms—how it benefits our health and happiness and how practices like the gratitude letter can help us cultivate it. But most of the evidence for this comes from studying Americans—and, specifically, the white American college students who are most likely to be recruited on the campuses where researchers work. Much less research has been conducted with participants from other cultural backgrounds, which creates a bias in the science. What we know about gratitude may not be so universal.

That's what researcher Acacia Parks discovered when she assigned students to write gratitude letters. One Asian-American student reported that her parents were insulted by her letter—as if it implied that she didn't expect them to be so generous. As Atieh Farashaiyan and Tan Kim Hua explain in a 2012 study contrasting gratitude in Iranian and Malaysian students, in some cultures, "giving thanks to family members or close friends for favors breaches the feeling of closeness since it is the responsibility of family members and close friends to assist each other."

That's why more and more researchers are exploring what gratitude looks and feels like in a range of cultures, from Brazil to Russia. This is a new frontier for the field, with few solid conclusions to date but lots of intriguing questions. Researchers are studying how children and adults worldwide naturally say thank-you and whether we can teach them to enhance their gratitude skills. The findings reveal the richness of this fundamental human experience—appreciating the kind things that other people do for us—that isn't always apparent in studies that focus on American participants. And they offer insights into how we can spread gratitude around a diverse world.

Different Ways We Say Thanks

Jonathan Tudge, a professor at the University of North Carolina at Greensboro, is perhaps the foremost expert on cultural differences in gratitude. When he first started exploring the topic ten years ago, he found virtually no existing research. He's since done many studies examining how gratitude emerges across different cultures. In one such study, which was discussed in chapter 3, Tudge and his colleagues explored how kids express gratitude in the United States, Brazil, Guatemala, Turkey, Russia, China, and South Korea. They found some similarities across cultures, but they also found some differences—an initial glimpse at how our early steps toward gratefulness might be shaped by larger societal forces.

In this study, kids ages seven to fourteen were asked to imagine what they would do for the person who granted their greatest wish. Overall, children in China and South Korea tended to favor connective gratitude—giving gifts that were meaningful to recipients, like making a favorite snack for a sibling. Meanwhile, kids in the United States leaned toward concrete gratitude, like giving a parent a toy—a gift the child likes, but mom may not. Children in Guatemala, where it's common to say "Thanks be to God" in everyday speech, were particularly partial to verbal gratitude.

Such variations in how children respond to kindness may set the stage for how they talk, act, and feel when they get older—and other research does find that adults give thanks differently worldwide.

In one study, Vajiheh Ahar and Abbas Eslami-Rasekh asked American and Iranian college students what they would say if they received different types of help, like someone holding a door, carrying their luggage, fixing their computer, or writing them a recommendation letter. The researchers observed a number of differences between the students' responses in the two countries.

The Americans were more likely than the Iranians to simply say thank-you, compliment the person ("What a gentleman!"), or promise compensation ("If you ever need anything, let me know"). Indeed, other research suggests that Americans (and Italians, too) are inveterate thankers, expressing gratitude in many everyday situations where people from other cultures simply do not. Meanwhile, the Iranian students used a variety of different strategies, depending on what the favor was and whether their helper had higher status than them (another study showed that Malaysians take this into account, as well). In particular, they were more likely than the Americans to acknowledge the favor ("You did me a great favor"), apologize for the imposition ("Sorry"), or ask God to reward the person. Clearly, gratitude comes in different flavors—and it seems that the roots of these variations begin in childhood.

How Culture Shapes Our Thanks

Why don't we all express gratitude in the same way? Cultural values, parenting practices, and education may each play a role. If you're an American adult, you may remember gluing together pasta ornaments or painting hand-shaped turkeys as holiday gifts for your parents, a form of the concrete gratitude that is so common among US kids. American culture tends to be very individualistic, in contrast with collectivist cultures that put much more emphasis on the social group. This is an important distinction, because (despite their underrepresentation in gratitude research) 85 percent of the world's population lives in cultures that researchers deem as more collectivist. In such cultures, people put greater emphasis on harmony and honoring others—values that would support the connective gratitude we see more in China and South Korea, which pays back kindness with things others might actually want (as opposed to things the giver deems most meaningful). In fact, one study found that the more respect Chinese children show to parents, the more grateful the kids tend to be.

But Tudge and others have argued that separating societies into individualist versus collectivist is too broad, reducing the colorful diversity of the world into two rigid categories. Instead, they prefer to consider at least two other dimensions of culture: autonomy/heteronomy and separateness/relatedness. In autonomous cultures, children are taught to be more independent and self-directed, whereas children in heteronomous cultures learn the duty to be obedient to parents and elders. Cultures that emphasize relatedness put greater value on connecting with others and developing relationships, which is less important to those that value separateness, or individuality.

These two dimensions can be crossed to yield four different types of cultures. Under this (still admittedly simplistic) schema, countries like the United States would be described as autonomous-separate, whereas rural areas in developing countries would be heteronomous-related, researchers posit. But urban areas in developing countries, like China or India, would tend to be more autonomous-related, as big cities offer a competitive environment where people can pursue more education and opportunities for themselves. Theoretically, autonomous-related societies would be the ones that are most supportive of authentic gratitude, since people would want to strengthen their relationships but would do so freely rather than out of a sense of obligation. True gratitude, after all, is not the polite thank-you uttered to avoid seeming rude but a genuine wish to pay back the undeserved blessings you receive.

Who Benefits from Gratitude Practices?

So far, we've looked at how children and adults in different societies naturally develop and express gratitude. But what happens when you try to teach people to be more grateful? Who benefits? This was the question behind a 2011 study where researchers invited Anglo-American and Asian-American people to try writing gratitude letters to their friends and family. Each week, some people wrote for ten minutes about their appreciation, and others simply wrote about what they had done that week. All participants in the study also reported how satisfied they were with life. After six weeks of the gratitude-writing exercise, the Anglo-American participants saw a boost in their well-being, as previous research would have predicted. But the Asian-American participants did not; their satisfaction with life barely changed. Similar studies have found that Indian and Taiwanese participants don't feel more grateful after writing gratitude letters and that South Korean students get a smaller well-being boost after writing gratitude letters than their American counterparts.

Why don't Asian and Asian-American participants see the same benefit that Anglo-Americans see from this practice? Expressing appreciation for other people's help may generate more mixed emotions for them, like indebtedness, guilt, and regret. In a recent study led by Liudmila Titova, for example, Indian people who wrote about their gratitude did feel more positive emotions, but they also felt more guilt and sadness—feelings absent in Anglo-American participants. The guilt they carried was mirrored in their writings, which more often talked about feeling in debt. For example, one person wrote that the "only thing which always pulls me down is that I could have given some gift as a token of gratitude."

Some cultures simply put more emphasis on that which we owe to others—so much so that gratitude can sometimes feel unnecessary or, as we saw earlier, even offensive, as if kindness were unexpected. "Giving and receiving help is an expected part of daily life for members of collectivist cultures, rather than an uplifting surprise, as may be the case for those from individualist cultures," write researcher Lilian J. Shin and her colleagues in their study.

Gratitude's Unexplored Territory

One might be tempted to conclude that gratitude is just not as important for Asian cultures. But recall that young Chinese and South

Korean children are particularly skilled at connective gratitude, which goes beyond polite words to reciprocate in a way that is meaningful to the helper. According to Tudge, this is the closest to authentic gratitude that kids can come. Might that suggest that, in fact, gratitude is more integral to Asian cultures than to others?

Scientists can't say for sure. It's likely that we don't understand the best ways to teach or even show gratitude in different cultural contexts yet. "Cultures as varied as the Japanese, the Inuit, and the Tamils of South India have developed entirely different ways of dealing with the receipt of gifts," write researcher Dan Wang and his colleagues. In Japan, it's vital to repay a gift with one that's at least as valuable as the one you were given. In Inuit culture, though, receiving a gift of meat after a hunt is par for the course, and it doesn't require an expression of gratitude at all. Meanwhile, in Tamil culture, nonverbal expressions of gratitude are common and easy, but verbal expressions of gratitude are difficult, in sharp contrast to how easy it is to say "thanks" in, for instance, the United States.

Researchers tout gratitude letters as a self-improvement exercise, to boost your mental and physical health. But this pitch may be less appealing outside of American culture with its strong emphasis on chasing personal goals and taking control of your life. That's why researchers are so careful about how they advertise an experiment, because they know that what people expect can influence their motivation, effort, and perception of the results. If researchers had sold gratitude as a way to strengthen relationships, for example, might participants have seen different outcomes?

Another complication is that these experiments all asked people to write gratitude letters, which simply might not be the ideal way to show gratitude in all cultures. Or it might matter whom we choose to express our gratitude toward. In the study where Indians were shown to feel more guilty, they were more likely to spontaneously focus their appreciation on people outside their family and even strangers, people whom they might feel obligated to repay for going out of their way to help.

To reduce these niggling negative feelings, Titova and her colleagues suggest that people from more collectivist cultures could be guided to think about the help they receive in a different way. "It might be possible to stave off indebtedness by encouraging participants to think of the target of their letter as having given their gifts freely, not expecting anything in return," they write.

What's clear is that gratitude deeply intersects with a culture's attitude about the self and its relation to others. Are we individuals forging our own paths or members of a larger whole? It's also true that this belief may vary from person to person; cultures are not monolithic. When children in the US say that their greatest wish is for someone else's well-being, their gratitude tends to become less concrete and self-focused and more connective and relationship promoting.

Gratitude is, after all, ultimately a skill that strengthens our relationships, and it arises when we pay more attention to our relationships and all the gifts they bring us. "At a time when the society seems to be more about me me me, we really need to get people thinking about connections," says Tudge. That means thinking about gratitude less like a good feeling to boost your happiness score and more like a moral virtue, the repayment and paying it forward of kindness that are part of being a good human being.

Continuing to study cultures beyond the United States—ones that acknowledge just how much our lives are enriched by our interdependence with others—may help us get at this deeper and more complex understanding of gratitude. Then we can learn how to make it a way of life.

CHAPTER 9

How Gratitude Builds Cooperation
By Eric Pedersen and Debra Lieberman

Gratitude seems to be very important for building and maintaining social relationships—that is, for how we come to value others. Along with our colleagues Michael McCullough, Daniel Forster, and Adam Smith, our recent research has examined how this underlying process works.

In one experiment, we told participants that they would be playing a computer game of catch with three other people (all of whom were secretly part of the research team). After meeting the other players face-to-face, the participants completed a survey that measured how much they valued their fellow players, by testing how willing they were to trade off their own welfare for that of the others.

By and large, we tend to be more willing to trade off our own welfare for (that is, help) people to whom we feel close. Under most circumstances, we are willing to expend more time and energy helping a family member or friend over an acquaintance, and an acquaintance over a stranger. The survey the study participants took measured their willingness to trade their welfare for that of another by generating a *welfare tradeoff ratio* (WTR). As you might expect, because the players were all strangers, initial levels of participants' WTR were quite low.

Next, the game of catch began. In this particular computer game, every time you threw the ball to the player who had been designated as the "Treasurer," you would win fifty cents. Needless to say, participants were hoping to get the ball and then have the opportunity to throw it to the Treasurer and rack up their earnings.

In some games, however, the Treasurer excluded the participant from the game, never throwing the ball back to them. After the other players played catch with the Treasurer for a number of rounds, something different happened: one of the other players began to throw the ball to the participant. That is, instead of throwing the ball to the Treasurer to increase their own winnings, this helpful player threw the ball to the participant so that they could earn some money—this player went out of their way to benefit them.

After the game, participants again completed a WTR survey for each of the other players to see how much they valued them. We also asked participants to rate how they felt about the other players on several dimensions—most notably, how grateful they were toward them. Finally, we had the participants play another economic game called the Dictator Game. In this one-move game, they were given ten dollars and told to allocate as much or as little as they wanted to the other players—an indication of cooperation.

Over the course of the study, we found three important patterns. First, as you might expect, participants valued the helpful player more after the first game. That is, WTRs increased for the player who helped the participant—and only this player. The WTRs for the other players either stayed the same or decreased.

Second, we found that increases in WTR predicted the level of gratitude the participant felt toward the helper. In other words, the greater the increase in how much participants valued the helper, the more gratitude they reported in response to that help.

Our third finding relates to cooperation. We found that participants allocated far larger percentages of money in the Dictator Game to the player who had helped them than to the other players who had not. But, unlike with gratitude, it wasn't the increase in WTR that predicted this cooperative behavior. Instead, it was the post-game WTR level—that is, how much participants now valued the welfare of that person.

This is a subtle but important distinction. *Increases*—that is, positive changes—in WTRs predicted gratitude, whereas *current* WTR values predicted giving above and beyond the effects of gratitude.

Gratitude seems to correspond to *positive changes* in how much we value others. When we express gratitude to someone, we are effectively signaling that, by virtue of their actions, we value them more than we did before. And if we value them more, we might be more likely to provide benefits to them in the future.

As an intensely social species, humans necessarily put great importance on establishing beneficial relationships with others, whether it be close friends, romantic partners, or work acquaintances. A major question, then, is how are we able to form cooperative relationships with others who aren't our immediate relatives? By signaling increases in WTR, gratitude may play a central role in the process by which strangers develop relationships that turn into friendships.

Generally speaking, we tend to feel grateful when a person does something nice for us—they delivered a benefit of some kind. As our experiment suggests, feelings of gratitude are explained by *how much more* we value our benefactor. Boiled down to their essence, the feelings of gratitude (and the psychological systems that cause these feelings) help identify likely cooperators—people who have demonstrated that they care and might continue to do so in the future. Our gesture or utterance of gratitude thus expresses to others that we've noticed their actions, we perceive them to be beneficial, and we might be potential reciprocators down the line.

When we detect expressions of gratitude from someone else, we are getting the same message. And hearing gratitude from someone might make us value them more, to the extent that we care about how our actions affect them—for instance, if we are looking to make a new friend. This is because, out of the sea of people in the world, this person has indicated that they value us and are thus more likely to be an ally. Therefore, helping this person in the future might have a better chance of bolstering a new, beneficial relationship than helping others who haven't demonstrated that they value us.

In this way, both detecting and expressing gratitude can create a snowball effect by ratcheting up mutual value, starting from the very first interaction and leading to a strong, cooperative relationship over time.

PART 3

How to Be Grateful

Gratitude is a social behavior—a prosocial one, to be specific—that strengthens our connections with other people, and our words make those connections visible. However, gratefulness is also a deeply private matter, a feeling that we must cultivate inside ourselves. This part of the book looks at the personal struggle to feel grateful, especially in the face of loss or hard times or bad feelings like guilt—or even just boredom.

Gratitude often comes to us spontaneously during the good times. We can feel naturally grateful for a great meal or critical help or the love of our spouse. But too many good meals, too much help, or quotidian grind can lead us to simply expect those things. In those cases, gratitude can be a tool—one among many—to wake up your mind and help you see the good things that you've been taking for granted.

That's hard enough, but gratitude can feel impossible when things aren't going well. When a loved one dies or we lose a job or we suffer a heart attack, gratitude doesn't feel like the right response—and yet, as several of our contributors argue, that is precisely when we need gratitude the most.

CHAPTER 10

How to Cultivate Gratitude in Yourself
By Jeremy Adam Smith

I'm terrible at gratitude. How bad am I? I'm so bad at gratitude that, most days, I don't notice the sunlight on the leaves of the Berkeley oaks as I ride my bike down the street. I forget to be thankful for the guy who hand-brews that delicious cup of coffee I drink midway through every weekday morning. I don't even know the dude's name! I usually take for granted that I have legs to walk on, eyes to see with, arms I can use to hug my son. I forget my son! Well, I don't actually forget about him, at least as a physical presence: I generally remember to pick him up from school and feed him dinner. But as I face the quotidian slings and arrows of parenthood, I forget all the time how much he's changed my life for the better.

As Robert Emmons describes in the first chapter of this book, gratitude (and its sibling appreciation) is the mental tool we use to remind ourselves of the good stuff. It's a lens that helps us see the things that don't make it onto our lists of problems to be solved. It's a spotlight that we shine on the people who give us the good things in life. It's a bright red paintbrush we apply to otherwise-invisible blessings, like clean streets or health or enough food to eat.

Gratitude doesn't make problems and threats disappear. We can lose jobs, we can be attacked on the street, we can get sick. I've experienced all those things. I remember those harrowing times at unexpected moments: my heart beats faster; my throat constricts. My body wants to hit something or run away, one or the other. But there's nothing to hit, nowhere to run. The threats are indeed real, but at that moment, they exist only in memory or imagination. *I am the threat.* I am the one who is wearing myself out with worry.

That's when I need to turn on the gratitude. If I do that enough, gratitude might just become a habit. What will that mean for me? According to the research, it means I increase my chances of psychologically surviving hard times, and I stand a chance of being happier in the good times. I'm not ignoring the threats that may come; I'm appreciating the resources and people that might help me face those threats.

If you're already one of those highly grateful people, stop reading this chapter—you don't need it. But if you're more like me, then here are some tips for how to become one of those fantastically grateful people. You'll find more specific, research-tested gratitude exercises at http://www.newharbinger.com/44611.

Once in a While, Think About Death and Loss

Didn't see that one coming, did you? I'm not just being perverse—contemplating endings really does make you more grateful for the life you currently have, according to several studies. For example, when Araceli Frias and colleagues asked people to visualize their own deaths, their gratitude measurably increased. Similarly, when Minkyung Koo and colleagues asked people to envision the sudden disappearance of their romantic partners from their lives, they became more grateful to their partners. The same goes for imagining that some positive event, like a job promotion, never happened.

This isn't just theoretical: when you find yourself taking a good thing for granted, try giving it up for a little while. Researchers Jordi Quoidbach and Elizabeth Dunn had fifty-five people eat a piece of chocolate—and then the researchers told some of those people to resist chocolate for a week and others to binge on chocolate if they wanted. They left a third group to their own devices.

Guess who ended up happiest, according to self-reports? The people who abstained from chocolate. And who were the least happy? The people who binged. That's the power of gratitude!

Take the Time to Smell the Roses

Grateful people also notice the fragrance of the coffee, the bread baking in the oven, the aroma of a new car—whatever gives them pleasure. Loyola University psychologist Fred Bryant finds that savoring positive experiences makes them stickier in your brain and increases their benefits to your psyche—and the key, he argues, is expressing gratitude for the experience. That's one of the ways appreciation and gratitude go hand in hand.

You might also consider adding some little ritual to how you experience the pleasures of the body: a study published in 2013 in *Psychological Science* finds that rituals like prayer or even just shaking a sugar packet to bring your attention to the beverage you're about to drink "make people pay more attention to food, and paying attention makes food taste better," as Emily Nauman reports in her *Greater Good Magazine* article about the research.

This brand of mindfulness makes intuitive sense, but how does it work with the first tip above? Well, we humans are astoundingly adaptive creatures, and we will adapt even to the good things in life. When we do, their subjective value starts to drop; we start to take them for granted. That's the point at which we might give them up for a while—be it chocolate, sex, or even something like sunlight—and then take the time to really savor them when we allow them back into our lives.

This applies to people in our lives, too, which goes back to the first habit: If you're taking someone for granted, take a step back—and imagine your life without them. Then try savoring their presence, just like you would a rose. Or a new car. Or whatever! The point is, absence may just make the heart grow grateful.

Take the Good Things as Gifts, Not as Your Birthright

What's the opposite of gratitude? Entitlement—the attitude that people owe you something just because you're so very special. "In all its manifestations, a preoccupation with the self can cause us to forget our benefits and our benefactors or to feel that we are owed things from others and therefore have no reason to feel thankful," writes Robert Emmons. "Counting blessings will be ineffective because grievances will always outnumber gifts."

The antidote to entitlement, argues Emmons, is to see that we did not create ourselves—we were created, if not by evolution, then by God; or if not by God, then by our parents. Likewise, we are never truly self-sufficient. Humans need other people to grow our food and heal our injuries. We need love, and for that, we need family, partners, friends, and pets.

"Seeing with grateful eyes requires that we see the web of interconnection in which we alternate between being givers and receivers," writes Emmons. "The humble person says that life is a gift to be grateful for, not a right to be claimed."

Be Grateful for People, Not Just Things

Sunlight and trees don't have feelings. Being grateful for them may have good effects, like leading you to think about your impact on the environment, but the trees don't care. Likewise, the sun doesn't know you exist; that big ball of flaming gas isn't even aware of its own existence, as far as anyone knows. Our gratitude doesn't make it burn any brighter.

That's not true of people—people will glow in gratitude, as several studies have found. Saying thanks to my son might make him happier, and it can strengthen our emotional bond. Thanking the guy who makes my coffee could strengthen our social bond—in part by deepening our understanding of how we're interconnected with other people. My colleague Emiliana Simon-Thomas, another codirector of the Greater Good Science Center's Expanding the Science and Practice of Gratitude project, put it to me this way: "Experiences that heighten meaningful connections with others—like noticing how another person has helped you, acknowledging the effort it took, and savoring how you benefited from it—engage biological systems for trust and affection, alongside circuits for pleasure and reward. This provides a synergistic and enduring boost to the positive experience. Saying thank-you to a person, your brain registers that something good has happened and that you are more richly enmeshed in a meaningful social community."

Mention the Pancakes

Grateful people are habitually specific. They don't say, "I love you because you're just so wonderfully wonderful, you!" Instead, the really skilled grateful person will say, "I love you for the pancakes you make when you see I'm hungry and the way you massage my feet after work, even when you're really tired, and how you give me hugs when I'm sad so that I'll feel better!" That is, they'll recognize specific things to be grateful for.

The reason for this is pretty simple: it makes the expression of gratitude feel more authentic, for it reveals that the thanker was genuinely paying attention and isn't just going through the motions. The richest thank-yous will acknowledge intentions ("the pancakes you make when you see I'm hungry") and costs ("you massage my feet after work, even when you're really tired"), and they'll describe the value of benefits received ("you give me hugs when I'm sad so that I'll feel better").

When Amie Gordon and colleagues studied gratitude in couples, they found that spouses implicitly express gratitude through more caring and attentive behavior. They ask clarifying questions; they respond to trouble with hugs and to good news with smiles. "These gestures," Gordon writes, "can have profound effects: participants who were better listeners during those conversations in the lab had partners who reported feeling more appreciated by them."

Remember: gratitude thrives on specificity!

Thank Outside the Box

Let's get real: pancakes, massages, hugs? Boring! Most of the examples, so far, are easy and clichéd. But here's who the really tough-minded grateful person thanks: the boyfriend who dumped her, the homeless person who asked for change, the boss who laid him off.

With this step, we're graduating from basic to advanced gratitude, so pay attention. And since I myself am still working on basic, I'll turn once again to Emmons, who writes, "It's easy to feel grateful for the good things. No one 'feels' grateful that he or she has lost a job or a home or good health or has taken a devastating hit on his or her retirement portfolio." In such moments, Emmons says, gratitude becomes a critical cognitive process—a way of thinking about the world that can help us turn disaster into a stepping-stone. If we're willing and able to look, that is, we can find a reason to feel grateful even to people who have harmed us. We can thank that boyfriend for being brave enough to end a relationship that wasn't working; the homeless person for reminding us of our advantages and vulnerability; the boss for forcing us to face new challenges. We can even give thanks in the face of death. As one participant in the Greater Good Science Center's online gratitude journal, Thnx4.org, wrote, "My dad recently passed away. I am so grateful to have had him in my life and to know that he cared tremendously for me. He wasn't shy about telling me how much he loved me. I will treasure those memories forever." In such a case, gratitude is a way to nurture the memory of someone we've lost.

This chapter described a few ways to feel and express gratitude. It's what truly, fantastically grateful people do. Can you?

How to Make the Most of
Your Gratitude Journal

By Alex Springer and Jason Marsh

There are specific ways to cultivate gratefulness, and journaling is one of the best documented.

There's no wrong way to keep a gratitude journal, but here is the basic idea: two or three times a week, write down up to five things for which you feel grateful. The things you list can be relatively small in importance ("the tasty sandwich I had for lunch today") or relatively large ("my sister gave birth to a healthy baby boy"). The goal of the exercise is to remember a good event, experience, person, or thing in your life and then enjoy the good emotions that come with it.

The physical record is important, though: don't just do this exercise in your head. You can write your thanks down in your own notebook, or you can do it on Thnx4.org, a free online platform created by the Greater Good Science Center. At Thnx4.org, participants can rate each gratitude experience on a scale from "made me momentarily smile" to "made my whole day glorious." When we analyzed four thousand such gratitude expressions posted between January and July of 2017, we asked, which forms of gratitude and which styles of gratitude journaling had more impact on the quality of a person's day?

Our findings confirmed some existing observations about the benefits of gratitude journaling, but we also noticed some interesting and new patterns, which may help you leverage the most from this gratitude practice:

Saying thanks aloud has the most positive impact on the thanker. Many more people reported a stronger positive impact on their day when they had actually said thank-you to the person to whom they felt grateful. It made a difference to say the words rather than just post them on Thnx4.org. If people did, they were significantly more likely to report that their experience of gratitude "made their whole day glorious."

Give public thanks for the good things people do, not things people buy. Anecdotal feedback suggests that publicly expressing gratitude for things—typically a fine possession, a lovely opportunity, or a privilege—can make other people unhappy, probably because it stimulates envy or just awareness of what they don't have. However, reading posts that describe people helping one another has the opposite effect: they often elevate and inspire readers and can even prompt the viral spread of gratitude.

Focus on love. Posts about feeling loved made the greatest positive impact. Of all the posts that people rated as having "made their day glorious," feeling loved, important, and appreciated was the most common theme. One user wrote, "M. made me a special sweet-and-sour pork dish when he was feeling poorly yesterday and brought me home some books because I'd said I wanted to read something good again. I had a lovely tea and felt very loved and cared about. It was so sweet."

Stick with it! Our analysis also showed that, over time, posts on Thnx4.org were rated as having more and more positive impact on users. So the longer you stick with your gratitude journaling routine, the better you'll feel. Why? We don't know for sure, but the data suggest that regularly writing about gratitude builds up a habit and enduring mood—an attitude of gratitude. Journaling helps us see others, ourselves, and our world through a thankful lens.

When Gratitude Exercises Feel Bad

By Megan M. Fritz and Sonja Lyubomirsky

Gratitude practices can sometimes elicit negative, rather than positive, emotions, thoughts, and behaviors. They may lead you to feel ashamed, incompetent, or inferior for having needed help in the first place or for not fulfilling your benefactor's expectations. Writing a letter of gratitude to someone who supported you could make you feel guilty or embarrassed for not having thanked the person sooner or could make you feel deeply indebted as the burden of needing to reciprocate sinks in.

Some of us have had the experience when the heartfelt sharing of gratitude was uncomfortable or awkward and hence made us feel less, rather than more, connected to the other person. These potential negative outcomes may cause those of us trying to become happier through gratitude activities to become paradoxically unhappier. Furthermore, gratitude expressions may not be received positively in all contexts. In East Asian cultures, for instance, an expression of gratitude may be viewed as burdensome (something you need to reciprocate), and parents may feel insulted for being thanked for doing something they consider to be part of their parental duty.

Why do these seemingly positive activities have negative consequences? It may be adaptive for certain practices to produce unpleasant feelings, particularly in the short term, in order to attain future rewards. In our work, we have proposed that gratitude can stimulate self-improvement by engendering enough positive emotion (feeling uplifted and supported by others) to motivate the person to approach their goals, but also enough negative emotion (feeling guilty and indebted) to recognize the need to do so.

For example, a college student might think, *Now that I recognize how hard my parents worked to support me throughout my education, I want to prove myself worthy of their sacrifices by being the best student possible.* The student's feelings of love for her parents, relief at being able to attend college, and hope for her future, paired with the subtle notion of guilt for her parents' sacrifices and embarrassment at not having achieved her best grades, may compose just the right emotional medley to energize her academic efforts. Future research may indeed find that small, brief backfiring effects are necessary for positive practices to produce gains in well-being in the long run.

All in all, research suggests that selecting positive activities that fit best with any of us as individuals—given our personality, interests, and values—will maximize the chances that such efforts catalyze well-being rather than backfire. And, in striving for greater happiness, it is crucial to keep in mind that the very behaviors that may sometimes seem to undermine such efforts, like writing a letter of gratitude to a mentor, are those that we need to harness to increase our happiness.

Five Ways Giving Thanks Can Backfire

By Amie Gordon

Although appreciating what you have—instead of lamenting what you have not—is generally good advice, it can backfire. How?

Overdosing on gratitude. When it comes to keeping track of your gratitude, the adage "more is better" doesn't necessarily apply. If you set too high a goal for your gratitude, you may find yourself falling short, which paradoxically could leave you feeling less grateful and happy than you would be if you hadn't tracked your gratitude at all. In a study of gratitude journaling, people who tracked their gratitude once per week were happier after six weeks than when they began, whereas those who tracked their gratitude three times per week were not. If you find yourself hesitating when putting pen to paper, you may begin to think your life isn't that good or you don't have that much to be grateful for. If that's the case, take a step back and focus on quality over quantity.

Focusing on feeling grateful for someone or something who isn't worthy. If you are in a bad relationship with someone who is emotionally or physically abusing you or who just can't make you happy, gratitude may be the wrong choice. By focusing on the ways that you appreciate your partner, boss, or roommate, you may choose to stay where you are, when you should be finding a way to get out of an unhealthy situation. Account for the entire relationship, not just the good parts!

Using gratitude to avoid a serious problem. Gratitude helps you focus on what is important instead of getting caught up in the little annoyances of everyday life. However, not all problems are little annoyances, and focusing your attention on things you appreciate may provide only temporary relief from serious problems. In fact, when it comes to serious problems, a negative emotion like anger may actually be more constructive. In one study of romantic couples, expressing anger was more beneficial than being positive, when discussing a severe problem, because the anger helped couples address and resolve the issue rather than sweep it under the rug.

Downplaying your own successes through excessive gratitude. After something good happens to you, you may only think about and thank the people who helped make it possible. But of equal importance is acknowledging your own role in the process. If you are someone who focuses on thanking everyone else, downplaying your own hard work and talent to a fault, you may be hiding low self-esteem behind your gratitude. Don't let gratitude for others get in the way of appropriately taking credit for your own part in success.

Mistaking gratitude for indebtedness. Gratitude is the positive emotion you feel when someone else helps you out. Indebtedness, on the other hand, generally leaves you with a bad taste in your mouth: someone helped you and now you feel you owe them. (Research suggests, though, that there are positive and negative versions of indebtedness. In some situations, indebtedness can sometimes make us more motivated to improve ourselves.) If you mistake feelings of gratitude for indebtedness, you may find yourself working hard to repay a favor—not to express your appreciation but to take the weight of a debt off your shoulders. In close relationships, this need to repay can actually lead to negative feelings between partners. Repaying someone who matters to you too quickly may be a sign that you don't want a close relationship. If you help a new romantic partner get groceries, for example, having them turn around the next day and do the same for you could feel too much like a tit for tat, when what you really want, in helping to get groceries, is recognition that you would like a more interdependent kind of relationship, where help is given out of generosity, not a desire for repayment.

CHAPTER 11

How to Say Thanks Without Feeling Indebted

By Jill Suttie

When we receive something from others, we don't *always* feel grateful. Instead of feeling grateful, we may feel indebted. Again, indebtedness is the condition of owing someone for something. It arises when we believe that something we've been given was perhaps cloaked in a hidden price tag or incurs obligation. Think of the boss who praises your work ethic or a certain friend who helped you move furniture. You may feel that you are expected to repay them in some way: the boss may expect you to work late; the friend might ask to borrow money and offhandedly remind you of that time he helped move the couch.

Research suggests that there are some important differences between the experiences of gratitude and indebtedness. For example, people who feel indebted tend to experience more negative emotions and feel stressed rather than uplifted, because they are worried about repayment. Indebtedness may also lead to less positive feelings about a benefactor and less inclination to want to help them out in the future.

There are many factors that can influence whether giving to another will elicit gratitude or indebtedness—or some combination of the two. Researchers have found feelings of gratitude and indebtedness can be affected by the relationship between giver and benefactor, the size of the gift, and the perceived intention of the giver—meaning, whether or not the receiver believes the giver is being benevolent or hoping to get something in return. In general, we tend to have more positive feelings associated with gratitude when the person giving to us is someone emotionally close to us, gives more generously, and is perceived to be acting out of benevolence. Science also suggests that some people may be more likely to feel indebted than others because of personal characteristics. For example, as Summer Allen describes in chapter 7, "How Gender Shapes Gratitude," some research has shown that men are more likely than women are to feel indebted when receiving an unexpected gift, perhaps because of societal values of independence and the myth of the self-made man. It's hard to feel grateful when doing so suggests you have others to thank for your success, which may explain why so many of my women friends complain about the lack of thanks they get from their husbands when they do something nice for them.

Culture also seems to play a role in whether or not we feel indebted, as Kira Newman describes in chapter 8. Again, some studies suggest that people from East Asian cultures are more likely to feel a combination of gratitude and indebtedness when receiving a gift, in part because of the cultural value placed on reciprocity. However, research suggests that even in East Asian cultures, gratitude rather than indebtedness is a more powerful motivator for building and maintaining social relationships.

If you want to say thanks without incurring the feeling of being indebted and, in turn, if you don't want others to feel indebted to you, here are four steps you can follow.

1. Keep the Focus on Others, Not Yourself

Just as with the pursuit of happiness, it's probably best to focus on others and your relationships when practicing gratitude—not on the potential benefits to yourself. Otherwise, you won't really be experiencing gratitude. "Gratitude is an *other*-focused emotion, where we're focused on what someone else has done for us," says gratitude researcher Philip Watkins. "If we focus on that, I think authentic gratitude naturally results."

Some research supports the importance of having an outward focus to avoid indebtedness. In one study, researchers found that someone with more of a self-focused attention in general will tend to experience indebtedness more than gratitude when receiving help or a gift. In another study, being more concerned with seeking safety and security in a relationship—a personal benefit—led participants to experience significantly less gratitude and more indebtedness than when their central concern was in nurturing a relationship, a more outwardly focused goal.

"The problem with the pop-psychology approach to gratitude is that we've emphasized happiness so much as the result of gratitude that we tend to focus on gratitude as a means to happiness," Watkins says. "It is. But when we're focusing on it as a means to happiness instead of what gratitude is in and of itself—appreciating what someone else has done for us—it's likely to backfire."

2. Practice Gratitude Even If You're Not Sure It's Totally Sincere

Why would we want to practice gratitude even when we're not exactly feeling it? Research seems to suggest that deliberate practices of gratitude don't just affect the naturally grateful but also those who don't enjoy gratitude practices or who tend to be more narcissistic. "In all the intervention studies I've done, they're always students doing it for course credit; but it still works," says Watkins. "We tend to emphasize that you really need to want to do gratitude to do it well. But you know what? Maybe not."

Does that mean we should encourage other people (like our children) to practice gratitude in some formal way? The answer is probably yes but with some important caveats. Children learn more from a parent who is modeling gratitude than from a parent who insists their kids "do what I say, not what I do," says Watkins.

Some research suggests that children can fairly easily be prompted to have a grateful mind-set, which leads to benefits like more positive emotion. Sitting down with a child and helping them think about the thoughtfulness of others or the sacrifices made on their behalf might prompt them to respond with more gratitude than simply putting them through their paces, says Watkins.

Still, Watkins suggests that we may want to avoid forcing it. For example, if we are practicing gratitude around the dinner table on Thanksgiving, it's probably best not to enforce strict turn-taking but to simply invite people to consider their blessings. Since gratitude, like other positive emotions, seems to be somewhat contagious, others may chime in anyway, creating a spiral of good feelings.

3. Give Gifts Freely, Without Strings Attached

What about when you're the one doing the giving? What can you do to prevent others from feeling indebted to you? When helping someone out or presenting them with a gift, it's important to give freely and without an expectation of getting something in return. If people think you are asking them to reciprocate in some way, or that you want them to feel obligated, they will be much less likely to feel grateful. Additionally, they will be less likely to want to give back to you or even to pay the generosity forward to someone else in their social network.

Luckily, the monetary cost of a gift is not that important for eliciting gratitude: what seems to matter is that you are thoughtful around your gift giving, taking the person's preferences and needs into account. Besides, giving gifts freely with a generous spirit is associated with many of its own rewards, including happiness. You will be more likely to enjoy the experience when you give without expectation. "Our research shows that if you give something to get something from a person, you're less likely to get something from them anyway—there's a reactive effect," says Watkins. "The joy of giving itself, rather than what the gift might get you from the person, needs to be the focus."

4. Stay Open to the Joy of Giving and Receiving

Gratitude naturally makes us feel good, both giving and receiving. But knowing how to nurture positive emotion in your life, in general—perhaps by taking a walk in nature, talking with a close friend, or listening to music—might help you create a spiral of good feelings that can lead to more gratitude and less indebtedness. Though the research on this is not definitive, there's some evidence to suggest that people who know how to savor positive emotions may be particularly prone to experiencing gratitude.

Practicing mindfulness meditation may help us be more attentive to the gifts in our lives as well as to the people who are responsible for providing them. Perhaps that is why mindfulness and gratitude are often promoted together and seem to interact for increasing well-being.

Watkins suggests that we can be more intentional around our gift-giving, as well. Too often, he says, we give because we're expected to do so, and we lose touch with the fact that giving is a choice. Instead of operating mindlessly, we can think about the other person and stay open to the joys of giving. "Just remembering that I don't have to do it, but I want to, and remembering to enjoy the act of giving itself," he says. "To me that's the key."

CHAPTER 12

Can Loss Make You More Grateful?

By Nathan Greene

My sister and I sat in my mother's bedroom—her sanctuary and prison, where cancer had kept her confined on and off for the past six years—as she looked out the window longingly. The stunningly sunny July day reminded her of everything she loved doing outdoors: tending to her roses, smelling the heads of strangers' babies, cheering for her children on the cross-country course.

She was getting cranky. Hindered by dry lips but motivated by restless legs, she pleaded in her best Jewish grandmother voice. "You guys have gotta get me out of here," she said, smiling coyly. "I'm dyin' in here…"

Morbid, Mom.

My sister and I exchanged a skeptical glance as we looked at the tubes and machinery she was connected to, the bag of nutrients that was keeping her alive, and considered the implausibility of any excursion. Though Mom clocked in at five-foot-two and under a hundred pounds, we knew a battle was fruitless; when she set her mind to an idea, we had no chance of stopping her.

A self-identified flower child who read Pema Chödrön and Thich Nhat Hanh, my mother fought two forms of cancer over sixteen years before her death. The disease took her hair, breasts, ovaries, fallopian tubes, and uterus, along with a third of her intestines. But her humanity grew. Following her first diagnosis when I was three, she and her closest friends championed a nonprofit called Healing Odyssey, a women's retreat for cancer survivors.

As odd as it may seem, I am a more grateful person today as a result of losing my mother. As I watched her fight with her everything to stay on this planet—to spend another day with my father, the love of her life, and to support my sister and me through our trials and triumphs— I began to value my life more. Of course, I had moments when I raged at the top of my lungs at cancer, and I'll never forget when the man from the morgue wheeled her body out of our house for the last time. But my appreciation for life also grew undeniably—and it led me to conduct research that would eventually explore how the death of a parent can inspire gratitude.

Nine years after my mother's death, I was studying loss, childhood trauma, and resilience for my doctorate (they call research "me-search," after all). I began wondering whether the experience of gratitude growing through loss might be universal. Early on, I came across a study that showed that our sense of gratitude can increase when we reflect in a personal way on our own death.

The authors of this study attributed the phenomenon to the *scarcity heuristic*, whereby we value things more when they are rare or scarce. So, when we're faced with death, the value we place on life rises. This was my experience. In witnessing my mom die at fifty-three, suddenly life felt very short, and each moment became incredibly important. I was excited to see my experience mirrored back to me in research, and inspired to study whether losing a parent in childhood made people more grateful.

Grateful After Loss

As a starting point, my colleague Katie McGovern and I asked 350 adults who had lost a parent about their gratitude, depression, psychological well-being, and *post-traumatic growth*—which is the positive change you can experience following a major personal crisis or traumatic experience—as well as how their gratitude changed as a result of the loss.

Unsurprisingly, we found that those who rated themselves higher in gratitude reported lower levels of depression and greater levels of psychological well-being and post-traumatic growth. In other words, the more grateful participants were faring better than those who were less grateful. Even more interesting, though, was that 79 percent of respondents believed that their experience of gratitude increased as a result of losing their parent; roughly 13 percent reported no change in gratitude, and only 8 percent reported that their sense of gratitude decreased.

Because this study was correlational, questions still remain as to whether these adults actually developed gratitude *because* of the loss or were already grateful to begin with. Also, it may have been difficult for people to accurately remember their gratitude levels prior to the loss. As such, we could only speak to their perceptions of changes in gratitude. Stronger evidence may come from a long-term study that observes how gratitude changes in children before and after losing a parent, compared to children who don't lose a parent.

Still, it was clear that a large majority of the adults in the study felt as I did—that losing their parent made them a more grateful person. To understand this in a more nuanced way, we invited people to write about their experience, and we analyzed the responses. The most common themes that people reported related to realizations that life is precious, feelings of gratitude for family and friends, and a recognition of impermanence. I was particularly moved by a quote from one woman in the study: "Losing my mother reminds me daily how precious life is and that I shouldn't take a single second for granted," she said. "From darkness, I eventually came into the light."

When Gratitude Is Hard

My mother was a wonderful, thoughtful person who tried as hard as she could to make hers a "good death." She joked about mortality and signed notes to us with "I love you eternally," part of a broad campaign to prepare my family for her death. She wrote letters to my sister and me to be opened on our wedding days, and she recorded herself on a Walkman reading our favorite childhood stories, so she could read to her grandbabies. As painful as it was to see my mother suffer over multiple years, we were given the gift of time. We held each other and laughed and cried together as much as we possibly could have in that period between diagnosis and death.

When I entered into my research about loss and gratitude, I wanted to acknowledge that not everyone who had lost a parent had experienced a "good death," as we had. They may not have had a close relationship with their parent, a parent who was so conscientious about preparing them for their death, or the opportunity to say good-bye. I didn't want the research to paint an unrealistically rosy picture or minimize the incredible pain that comes with loss. And the last thing I wanted was for those who were grieving to feel like they *should* be feeling grateful.

As a result, we also studied why it was challenging for some of the participants to access gratitude following the loss of a parent. We found, unsurprisingly, that those who experienced additional traumatic events in adulthood were struggling more. When people believed their sense of gratitude had decreased following the loss, they tended to attribute it to fear, anxiety, and a feeling that they couldn't depend on others.

I most certainly do not feel grateful every day. I become angry every Mother's Day and embarrassed about the envy I feel toward the beautiful connection my best friend has with her one-year-old son. In every accomplishment or milestone I reach, there is a tinge of melancholy—it serves as a reminder that the world has continued spinning without my mom in it.

In living with this incredible burden and gift of parental loss, no feelings are simple or singular. In the overwhelming wave of sadness that envelops my heart when I smell her perfume on a stranger or wake up from a dream in which she visits me, there is also a deep achy joy in feeling connected to her. This is the gift of grief: an opening to the complexity of moment-to-moment experience, which, for me, inevitably gives way to gratitude.

What Truly Matters

On that July day, we carefully guided Mom into the passenger seat of her yellow Volkswagen Beetle and drove to an overlook in Laguna Beach. Left arm clasped to mine and right arm clasped to my sister's, my mother shuffled down the pathway leading to the water. With a halt, she pointed out a crop of angel-wing jasmine. "You guys have to smell these," she coaxed, with that same look she would have in front of a piece of chocolate cake—eyes wide, guilty of an indulgence. I watched her as she closed her eyes, dipping her face into the small, star-shaped flowers and drinking in their scent as if they were a life force.

We continued down the path toward the edge of a cliff—a meeting place between two worlds—and pressed against the railing. The three of us stood, hand in hand, and our eyes softly closed as the sun warmed our skin. For the first time in the six years since she was diagnosed with ovarian cancer, our shoulders released. We breathed fully and calm swept over us.

"This is where spirituality lies," my mother said, with the surety of a new discovery. Staring death in the face and marveling at the supreme beauty of the universe, something in her had shifted. Her mama-bear stubbornness, her moments of confusion, anger, and sadness, were replaced by a calm acceptance. And my sister and I followed her lead.

Mom took us to the edge that day with her, to confront our own deaths as well as hers. In moments like this, what truly matters quickly shifts into focus; it becomes glaringly obvious that our time here is so finite and death can come at any moment. As the sea salt mist caressed our faces, we held each other tightly, in preparation for letting go.

Grief, Grace, and Gratitude

By Arianna Huffington

I've come to believe that living in a state of gratitude is the gateway to grace. Grace and gratitude have the same Latin root, *gratus*. Whenever we find ourselves in a stop-the-world-I-want-to-get-off mind-set, we can remember that there is another way and open ourselves to grace. And it often starts with taking a moment to be grateful for this day, for being alive, for anything.

I find that I'm not only grateful for all the blessings in my life but also grateful for all that hasn't happened—for all those close shaves with "disaster" of some kind or another, all the bad things that almost happened but didn't. The distance between them happening and not happening is grace.

And then there are the disasters that did happen, that leave us broken and in pain.

For me, such a moment was losing my first baby. I was thirty-six and ecstatic at the prospect of becoming a mother. But night after night, I had restless dreams. Night after night, I could see that the baby—a boy—was growing within me, but his eyes would not open. Days became weeks, and weeks turned into months. Early one morning, barely awake myself, I asked out loud, "Why won't they open?" I knew then what was only later confirmed by the doctors. The baby's eyes were not meant to open; he died in my womb before he was born.

Women know that we do not carry our unborn babies only in our wombs. We carry them in our dreams and in our souls and in our every cell. Losing a baby brings up so many unspoken fears: Will I ever be able to carry a baby to term? Will I ever be able to become a mother? Everything felt broken inside. As I lay awake during the many sleepless nights that followed, I began to sift through the shards and splinters, hoping to find reasons for my baby's stillbirth.

Staggering through a minefield of hard questions and partial answers, I began to make my way toward healing. Dreams of my baby gradually faded, but for a time it seemed as if the grief itself would never lift. My mother had once given me a quotation from Aeschylus that spoke directly to these hours: "And even in our sleep, pain which cannot forget falls drop by drop upon the heart, and in our own despair, against our will, comes wisdom to us by the awful grace of God." At some point, I accepted the pain falling drop by drop and prayed for the wisdom to come.

I had known pain before. Relationships had broken, illnesses had come, death had taken people I loved. But I had never known a pain like this. What I learned through it is that we are not on this earth to accumulate victories, or trophies, or experiences, or even to avoid failures, but to be whittled and sandpapered down until what's left is who we truly are. This is the only way we can find purpose in pain and loss, and the only way to keep returning to gratitude and grace.

I love saying grace—even silently—before meals and when I travel around the world, observing different traditions. When I was in Tokyo in 2013 for the launch of HuffPost Japan, I loved learning to say *itadakimasu* before every meal. It simply means "I receive." When I was in Dharamsala, India, every meal started with a simple prayer. Growing up in Greece, I was used to a simple blessing before each meal, sometimes a silent one, even though I wasn't brought up in a particularly religious household.

"Grace isn't something that you go for, as much as it's something you allow," wrote John-Roger Hinkins, the founder of the Movement of Spiritual Inner Awareness. "However, you may not know grace is present, because you have conditioned the way you want it to come, for example, like thunder or lightning, with all the drama, rumbling, and pretense of that. In fact, grace comes in very naturally, like breathing."

CHAPTER 13

How Gratitude Can Help You Through Hard Times

By Robert Emmons

Two decades' worth of research on gratitude has shown me that when life is going well, gratitude allows us to celebrate and magnify the goodness. But what about when life goes badly? I have often been asked if people can—or even should—feel grateful under dire circumstances. My response is that a grateful attitude will not only help but is also essential. In fact, it is precisely under crisis conditions when we have the most to gain by a grateful perspective on life. In the face of demoralization, gratitude has the power to energize. In the face of brokenness, gratitude has the power to heal. In the face of despair, gratitude has the power to bring hope. In other words, gratitude can help us cope with hard times.

Don't get me wrong. I am not suggesting that gratitude will come easily or naturally in a crisis. It's easy to feel grateful for the good things. But no one feels grateful for losing a job or a home or good health or a loved one. How can they? However, it is vital to make a distinction between *feeling* grateful and *being* grateful. We don't have total control over our emotions. We cannot easily will ourselves to feel grateful, less depressed, or happy. Feelings follow from the way we look at the world, thoughts we have about the way things are, the way things should be, and the distance between these two points. But being grateful is a choice, a prevailing attitude that endures and is relatively immune to the gains and losses that flow in and out of our lives. When disaster strikes, gratitude provides a perspective from which we can view life in its entirety and not be overwhelmed by temporary circumstances. Yes, this perspective is hard to achieve, but my research says it is worth the effort. We need to remember that gratitude is never a *should*, but always a *could*. Can we create gratefulness even in the midst of turmoil? I think you will find that more times than not, the answer is yes.

Remember the Bad

Trials and suffering can actually refine and deepen gratefulness if we allow them to show us not to take things for granted. Why? Well, when times are good, people take prosperity for granted and begin to believe that they are invulnerable. In times of uncertainty, though, people realize how powerless they are to control their own destiny. If you begin to see that everything you have, everything you have counted on, may be taken away, it becomes much harder to take it for granted.

So, crisis can make us more grateful—but research says gratitude also helps us cope with crisis. Consciously cultivating an attitude of gratitude builds up a sort of psychological immune system that can cushion us when we fall. There is scientific evidence that grateful people are more resilient to stress, whether minor everyday hassles or major personal upheavals. The contrast between simply suffering from a stressful experience and finding something in it to be grateful for— thereby redeeming it—serves as the basis for one of my tips for practicing gratitude: remember the bad.

It works this way: think of the worst times in your life, your sorrows, your losses, your sadness, and then remember that here you are, able to remember them, that you made it through the worst times of your life— you got through the trauma, you got through the trial, you endured the temptation, you survived the bad relationship, you're making your way out of the dark. Remember the bad things; then look to see where you are now.

This process of remembering how difficult life used to be and how far we have come sets up an explicit contrast that is fertile ground for gratefulness. Our minds think in terms of *counterfactuals*—mental comparisons between the way things are and how things might have been different. Contrasting the present with negative times in the past can make us feel happier (or at least less unhappy) and enhance our overall sense of well-being. This opens the door to coping gratefully.

Try this little exercise. First, think about one of the unhappiest events you have experienced. Then ask yourself how often you find yourself thinking about this event today. Does the contrast with the present make you feel grateful and pleased? Do you realize your current life situation is not as bad as it could be? Try to realize and appreciate just how much better your life is now. The point is not to ignore or forget the past but to develop a fruitful frame of reference in the present from which to view experiences and events.

There's another way to foster gratitude: confront your own mortality, as Jeremy Adam Smith playfully suggests in chapter 10. In one study, researchers asked a group of participants to imagine a scenario where they are trapped in a burning high-rise, overcome by smoke, and killed. This resulted in a substantial increase in gratitude levels, as researchers discovered when they compared this group to people in two control conditions who were not compelled to imagine their own deaths.

In these ways, remembering the bad can help us appreciate the good. As the German theologian and Lutheran pastor Dietrich Bonhoeffer once said, "Gratitude changes the pangs of memory into a tranquil joy." We know that gratitude enhances happiness, but why? Gratitude maximizes happiness in multiple ways, and one reason is that it helps us reframe memories of unpleasant events in a way that decreases their unpleasant emotional impact. This implies that grateful coping entails looking for positive consequences of negative events. For example, grateful coping might involve seeing how a stressful event has shaped who you are today and has prompted you to reevaluate what is really important in life.

Of course, to say that gratitude is a helpful strategy to handle hurt feelings does not mean that we should try to ignore or deny suffering and pain. But the practice of gratitude does help us here, too.

Reframing Disaster

The field of positive psychology has at times been criticized for failing to acknowledge the value of negative emotions. Barbara Held of Bowdoin College in Maine, for example, contends that positive psychology has been too negative about negativity and too positive about positivity. To deny that life has its share of disappointments, frustrations, losses, hurts, setbacks, and sadness would be unrealistic and untenable. Life involves suffering. No amount of positive thinking exercises will change this truth.

So, telling people who are suffering to simply buck up, count their blessings, and remember how much they still have to be grateful for can certainly do much harm. But processing a life experience through a grateful lens does not mean denying negativity. It is not a form of superficial happiology. Instead, it means realizing the power you have to find opportunities in the obstacles you face. It means reframing a loss into a potential gain, recasting negativity into positive channels for gratitude. Gratefulness is not circumstantial or conditional on what is happening. It is a stance that one takes toward life, and difficulties are inevitable and unavoidable in life.

A growing body of research has examined how grateful recasting works. In a study conducted at Eastern Washington University, participants were randomly assigned to one of three writing groups that would recall an unpleasant open memory—a loss, a betrayal, victimization, or some other personally upsetting experience. The first group wrote for twenty minutes on issues that were irrelevant to their open memory. The second wrote about their experience pertaining to their open memory.

Researchers asked the third group to focus on the positive aspects of a difficult experience—and discover what about it might now make them feel grateful. Participants were never told to avoid thinking about the negative aspects of the experience or to deny or ignore the pain. Results showed that this group demonstrated more closure and less unpleasant emotional impact than participants who just wrote about the experience without being prompted to see ways it might be redeemed with gratitude. Moreover, those who found reasons to be grateful demonstrated fewer intrusive memories, such as wondering why it had happened, whether it could have been prevented, or whether they believed they caused it to happen. Thinking gratefully, this study showed, can help heal troubling memories and, in a sense, redeem them—a result echoed in many other studies.

Some years ago, I asked people with debilitating physical illnesses to compose a narrative concerning a time when they felt a deep sense of gratitude to someone or for something. I asked them to let themselves re-create that experience in their minds so that they could feel the emotions as vividly as though they had transported themselves back in time to the event itself. I also had them reflect on what they felt in that situation and how they expressed those feelings. In the face of progressive diseases, people often find life extremely challenging, painful, and frustrating. I wondered whether it would even be possible for them to find anything to be grateful about. For many of them, life revolved around visits to the pain clinic and pharmacy. I would not have been at all surprised if resentment overshadowed gratefulness.

As it turned out, most respondents had trouble settling on a specific instance—they simply had so much in their lives that they were grateful for. I was struck by the profound depth of feeling that they conveyed in their essays and by the apparent life-transforming power of gratitude in many of their lives.

It was evident from reading these narrative accounts that

1. Gratitude can be an overwhelmingly intense feeling.

2. Gratitude for gifts that others easily overlook can be the most powerful and frequent form of thankfulness.

3. Gratitude can be chosen in spite of one's situation or circumstances.

I was also struck by the redemptive twist that occurred in nearly half of these narratives: out of something bad (suffering, adversity, affliction) came something good (new life or new opportunities) for which the person felt profoundly grateful.

Of course, the unpleasant experiences in our lives don't have to be of the traumatic variety for us to gratefully benefit from them. If you are troubled by an open memory or a past unpleasant experience, whether it's a large or small event, you might consider trying to reframe how you think about it, using the language of thankfulness. Here are some questions to ask yourself:

- *What lessons did the experience teach me?*

- *Can I find ways to be thankful for what happened to me now, even though I was not at the time it happened?*

- *What ability did the experience draw out of me that surprised me?*

- *How am I now more the person I want to be because of it?*

- *Have my negative feelings about the experience limited or prevented my ability to feel gratitude in the time since it occurred?*

- *Has the experience removed a personal obstacle that previously prevented me from feeling grateful?*

Remember, your goal here is not to relive the experience but rather to get a new perspective on it. Simply rehearsing an upsetting event makes us feel worse about it. That is why catharsis has rarely been effective. Emotional venting without accompanying insight does not produce change. No amount of writing about the event will help unless you are able to take a fresh, redemptive perspective on it. This is an advantage that grateful people have—and it is a skill that anyone can learn.

PART 4

How to Be a Grateful Family

Family can mean many different things. It can look like parents and children and grandparents and uncles and cousins. Some families have just one biological parent; in many, the parents live in two different homes. In those families and in others, children might have an extended network of adults who love and take care of them. People also form chosen families from networks of friends. These aren't mutually exclusive categories; different kinds of families can and do combine.

Whatever family means to you, research suggests that gratitude will help yours thrive. There are, however, some special challenges to cultivating gratitude within families. We're quick to take family members for granted. Because these relationships are so close and go back so far, our feelings about family members can become complicated as bad memories mingle with sincere feelings of love.

This part of the book explores how to cultivate gratitude between intimate partners, in children, and within extended families. It starts with the fundamental unit of two people and then expands to discuss integrating gratitude in the whole family. Two very personal essays illustrate how some of the abstract principles described in this book operate in the lives of actual people. In other words, at this point in the book, we're getting down to brass tacks. Gratitude is more than an idea that comes down from an ivory tower. As these personal essays reveal, gratitude can also be a struggle to achieve.

CHAPTER 14

Why Couples Need to Thank Each Other

By Jess Alberts and Angela Trethewey

Q: *Are you grateful for your partner's household labor?*

Him: Uh, yeah, I guess so.

Q: *How do you express it?*

Him: She just knows.

—From a focus group conducted by the authors

The division of household labor is one of the most frequent sources of conflict in romantic relationships. As researchers Philip and Carolyn Cowan have shown, when partners feel that the division of labor (a combination of housework and paid work) in their relationship is unfair, they are more dissatisfied with their marriage and more likely to think they would be better off divorced. However, even an equitable division of labor may not be enough to ensure that partners are satisfied with their relationship.

As sociologist Arlie Hochschild and others have argued, a successful relationship depends not just on how partners divide labor but also on how they each express gratitude for the labor the other one contributes. This can be as true for single-income couples as for dual-income ones. When you perform work around the house—from cooking to laundry to checking your kids' homework—it often feels like a burden to you and a gift to your partner. So, if you don't feel that your partner is grateful for your efforts, especially if you perform the lion's share of domestic labor, that's likely to exacerbate feelings of inequity and dissatisfaction, making a difficult situation even worse.

In our research, we set out to test this theory—that it's not just the division of labor but also the expression of gratitude that's key to a strong and lasting relationship. Through focus groups, interviews, and surveys with people in heterosexual and same-sex relationships, we've found evidence that gratitude isn't just a way to mitigate the negative effects of an unequal division of labor. Rather, a lack of gratitude may be connected to why that division of labor is so unequal to begin with.

Fortunately, through our research, we've started to understand how couples can identify different reasons behind their unbalanced workloads and achieve more equity in their division of labor, cultivating a greater sense of fairness, satisfaction, and gratitude in their relationships.

Why Doesn't He See It?

Her: The house is a wreck! Why didn't you put a load of laundry in the wash, put the dishes in the dishwasher, or just take out the garbage that's overflowing?

Him: I didn't notice.

We have found that this conversation resonates with virtually all of our research participants—whether the complainer or the complained about. Complainers say, incredulously, "How can they not see it?" Their partners claim earnestly that they really didn't notice the mess and don't understand why their partners are so upset. To make matters worse for the complainers, their unaware partners not only fail to notice the dirty windows, piles of laundry, or overflowing garbage but also don't even notice when someone else takes care of these problems.

Although gender is a strong predictor of who will perform household labor (conservative estimates suggest women perform two-thirds of all household tasks, not including child care), it isn't entirely clear why women take on this burden even in cases where they earn 50 percent or more of a family's income. Our research suggests one of the keys to determining who will perform a specific household task is each partner's *response threshold*, which describes the degree of disorder that must exist before someone is sufficiently bothered to perform a task that's not being done. Individuals with low response thresholds for a specific task are moved to perform the task earlier than those who have a higher threshold.

Interestingly, this theory is originally based on studies of social networks and division of labor among ants and bees. In her research, entomologist Jennifer Fewell found that certain bees were almost always the ones to take action once the level of honey in the hive had dropped to a particular level. In addition, she discovered that their work reduced the chance that other, higher-threshold bees would perform the job in the future.

We've all seen the same dynamics play out among humans. For example, if Joan's partner Ted is disturbed when the trash in the wastebasket approaches the rim, whereas it doesn't bother her until the trash spills onto the floor, Ted will take out the trash before Joan is moved to do so. If the difference in their disturbance levels is great enough, Joan will never empty the trash, because Ted will always take care of it before it bothers her, possibly before she ever even notices the garbage.

What's more, if one partner does something well, that increases the chance they'll perform that task again, just as failing at the task (or a lack of opportunity to complete it) decreases the chance they'll get another turn. Before long, the partner who performs a task more frequently will likely be seen as a specialist at it. Taken together, these factors explain how one partner can get stuck with a household chore. (Of course, people are not bees or ants. Men and women are socialized differently, and part of that socialization includes different response thresholds.)

Consider Cristina and Stephen: Cristina began doing the laundry because she had a lower threshold for piles of dirty clothes, but through repetition, she became an "expert" at laundry, and, ultimately, she and Stephen came to see the task as "hers." Partners may have different thresholds for many (or even most) tasks. If one partner's threshold level for tasks around the house is consistently lower than the other's, then that first partner will take on a greater share of the housework. They might be able to tolerate this imbalance if their partner appreciated their extra work, but too often it's taken for granted.

Why Isn't She Grateful?

Her: So that roommate that I had last year was horrible. She never thanked me for anything, she never cleaned the house—it was horrible. Yeah, I wouldn't live with her again.

Hochschild's theory of "the economy of gratitude" explains why underperformers often aren't grateful for their partner's efforts and don't pitch in their fair share. Hochschild argues that, in relationships, "gifts" are understood as something extra, beyond what is expected. On the flip side, the stuff that isn't a gift is expected, and it goes unnoticed. Therefore, if the laundry (or trash, or dishes, or all of the above) is defined as "yours," then your partner is unlikely to feel gratitude toward you for doing it. After all, you are just doing what you are "supposed" to do, what you are "so much better" at doing. In fact, your partner may argue, since the undone task bothers you, you aren't doing it for them, but for yourself. Thus, your partner is unlikely to feel gratitude— because they don't view your efforts as a gift.

In terms of the division of labor, then, household partners often develop this pattern: the person with the lower response threshold performs tasks before their partner is moved to do so; the tasks come to be defined as "theirs"; the partner does not feel responsible for performing the task—and does not feel grateful, because the overperformer is just doing "their" job—all of which makes the partner less likely to lend a hand in the future.

Now, here's the good news: gratitude can help alter the dynamics of couples' division of labor. Expressing gratitude reminds the under-performing partner that the division of labor is not fair, and that their partner's contributions are a gift. And since people who receive gifts typically feel obligated to reciprocate, this insight can lead the under-performing partner to offer gifts of their own by contributing more to household tasks. In addition, the overperforming partner is likely to experience less resentment and frustration once their efforts are recognized and appreciated.

The economy of gratitude, then, helps explain the fact that husbands and wives are most satisfied in their marriages when they perceive that their spouses do more than their fair share of the work. That is, when you view your partner's household labor as a gift, over and above what is expected, then you are grateful and happy in the marriage. And, in turn, we have found that people who feel appreciated by their partners do indeed express less resentment over the division of labor and greater satisfaction with their relationships than do other study participants.

Appreciating Gifts

So how can couples bring all these pieces together into greater satisfaction with their relationships? Part of the answer comes from simply being aware of these dynamics. Once you accept that, in a sense, your partner may truly not have seen the dirty dishes, piles of laundry, and overflowing garbage, you will tend to be less angry and can discuss the issue more calmly and in a less accusatory fashion—which, in turn, can help your partner be less defensive.

That said, it's often even better to anticipate problems before they arise. Overperformers should avoid repetitively performing a task they don't want to own, especially when they're first living with their partner. In other words, when you first move in together, be careful not to cook dinner every night—or you might expect to continue cooking it every night for the rest of your relationship. Take turns in the beginning so that you can both own the task down the line.

Overperformers who are trying to break a cycle can also communicate to their partner when a task should be performed rather than waiting for the partner's threshold level to be reached—and resenting them for their lack of awareness. If an underperformer who is trying to do more around the house does not perform a task to their partner's standards, statements of appreciation—rather than criticism for not doing it right or for doing it too late—are more likely to encourage improvement.

It also helps if underperformers understand that their partner is more disturbed by a messy house, and they recognize the need to develop strategies to respond to this difference in threshold levels, such as performing a task regardless of whether it seems necessary. Each partner can take responsibility for specific tasks that they perform on a schedule—for instance, by taking out the garbage every Monday and Thursday—whether or not they think it needs to be done right then.

Finally, domestic partners may find it helpful to write down a list of their tasks and then switch lists for a week or a month to better understand their partner's contributions. They may be surprised to discover their partner does far more than they thought. When her husband Jim was on crutches for two weeks, one of us (Jess) discovered that she did, in fact, perform more routine household labor, but she also discovered that Jim typically performed many of the "dirty" tasks that she really didn't want to do. She then began to see their division of labor as more equitable.

The gratitude issue is thornier. But understanding the role of gratitude in the division of labor can encourage overperformers to take responsibility for fewer tasks so that these tasks are not taken for granted as belonging to the other person. Also, understanding the economy of gratitude can help underperformers recognize that they do benefit from their partner's efforts—that this work is, in fact, a gift to them, wrapped in clean laundry and vacuumed rugs. They might not be disturbed by disorder as early as their partners are, but eventually they would be, and they would have to do the tasks themselves. Thus, their partners are performing tasks that, rightly, belong to both of them. And if partners practice some of the steps outlined above to create a more equitable division of labor, they're likely to gain newfound appreciation for the work the other person performs for them.

It's unlikely that these suggestions will eliminate conflict around couples' division of labor. But we do believe that they can help partners reduce the frequency of their conflict, increase their expressions of gratitude, and improve their overall feelings about their relationship. Most of all, they can help partners avoid the trap of taking each other for granted, and start to appreciate all the gifts—big and small—that they give to each other.

How to Say Thank-You to Your Partner

By Sara Algoe

In my research, I've invited couples in romantic relationships to come into the laboratory and thank their partner for something—with video cameras rolling. Everyone expressed their gratitude in different ways. Some conversations were long, some short, some about important or seemingly unimportant things. After the conversation in the lab, we asked the benefactor—the person who did the kind thing and received the gratitude—to privately report on how the conversation went. We asked how responsive the grateful person was; we also asked how good the benefactor felt after hearing the expression, by having them rate their emotions.

Mentioning benefits to yourself and praising your partner's actions are both positive expressions, and different people used one, the other, or both—they were independent from one another. But our research shows that mentioning benefits to yourself is not as important—it can be there or not—as praising your partner's actions. The expressions of gratitude that leave the biggest impact are sure to acknowledge what it was about the partner's actions that stood out as praiseworthy.

Specifically, benefactors did not have more positive feelings after hearing the grateful person elaborate more on how much they loved the gift—or see the grateful partner as being more responsive—it simply didn't matter. However, when grateful people called out the praiseworthiness of their partner's actions, their partners perceived them as being more responsive and were in a better mood.

In other words, the most impactful expressions of gratitude emphasize the *you* in thank-you. Collectively, my team's work from these studies and those of others in the field suggest the following takeaways:

If you feel grateful, don't forget to show it. Saying anything, even a simple thank-you, can incidentally bring rewards for you and your partner. Expressing gratitude simultaneously makes your partner feel valued and—with very little effort—makes it clear that you are worth their investment. This might seem like an obvious suggestion, but life gets in the way and we sometimes forget to say something or second-guess whether we should. It's fine to just keep it simple, but if the spirit moves you, go for it.

If you are going to elaborate, don't forget to put the *you* in thank-you. The couples in these studies took the time to sit down and have a face-to-face conversation with their partner. That might be nice to do, but you don't even have to go that far. In real time, as the feeling of gratitude unfolds, or even in a written thank-you note, you can add a simple line to call out what it was about the person's actions that stood out to you the most.

Be sincere and appropriate to the situation and relationship. In the studies I described above, the benefits to the benefactor hearing the thank-you were contingent on seeing their partner as caring, understanding, and validating. Going over the top when it's unwarranted may actually undermine an expression by making it seem insincere. No need to overdo it.

Why Men Need to Learn Gratitude

By Jeremy Adam Smith

As Summer Allen argues in "How Gender Shapes Gratitude" in part 2, the research suggests that men are worse than women when it comes to being grateful. This makes for an emotionally lethal combination: tradition imposes housework and child care on women, and then individual men aren't grateful for their wives' contributions, a habit that might have a lot to do with maintaining their own social power or just being blind to the amount of power they have.

One 2011 study by Yeri Cho and Nathanael J. Fast paired two participants and asked them to perform a task together, designating one the supervisor and the other the subordinate. The results have useful implications for marriages. They found that gratitude from supervisors made subordinates happier, of course. But they also found that supervisors who had been challenged in any way by their subordinates were more likely to turn around and insult that person.

How might this play out in marriages? In a 2012 study, M. Ena Inesi and colleagues ran five experiments testing how power shapes gratitude. They found that people with power were less likely to express gratitude to people with less power; people with power also, cynically, tended to believe others thanked them mainly to curry favor down the line, not out of authentic feeling. In marriages, this gratitude corruption also led to lower levels of marital commitment in the more powerful spouse.

A 2013 study by psychologist Amie Gordon and colleagues found that people who tested low in gratitude would be even less empathic "after they thought about a time when they had a lot of power in their relationship." However, "More grateful people reported being better perspective-takers regardless of their power."

In other words, gratitude seems to inoculate people against the antisocial effects of feeling powerful.

The bottom line from these and similar experiments is clear. Power imbalances worsen relationships, but expressing gratitude can help break vicious cycles and even change the balance of power.

For me as a man, this amounts to a persuasive feminist argument. Power inequalities cut us off from genuine and necessary human feelings like gratitude, and that can push us a little further away from the possibility of happiness. It's the role of the spouse to serve as witness to their partner's life. Gratitude tells the spouse that they are being seen, that their sacrifices and struggles are visible and honored. If we're not doing that, we're failing each other.

We can act against power imbalances through our votes and political activism. It's policies like flextime and paid parental leave that will best help women advance in their careers. But we can also make a small, positive contribution in our own homes by just saying thanks. Even if we can't have it all—all relationships involve some degree of compromise between partners, by their very nature—we can at least help each other appreciate what we have.

How Gratitude Can Help Couples Through Illness

By Jill Suttie

Caretaking for someone who is injured or sick can be a challenge, but it's especially charged when their needs are frequent and long term. A caregiver may feel obligated to help, but doing so may bring little joy or sense of meaning, making it hard to sustain. And it can be equally stressful for the receiver of care, because they might feel themselves to be a burden to their caregiver.

How can couples improve this dynamic? New research suggests that what motivates people to help is crucial and that motivation is affected by both their interactions with the person they're caring for and their life outside caregiving. Researchers who study motivation identify two basic types: *autonomous* or *intrinsic motivation*, when you do something because it brings you joy, satisfaction, or meaning, and *controlled* or *extrinsic motivation*, when you do something out of loyalty or because you'd feel guilty if you didn't do it. Either way, you end up helping, but autonomous motivation feels better and leads to better outcomes.

Researchers have found that caregivers who had more intrinsic motivation to help their sick partners felt happier, more satisfied with their relationship, and less distressed about caregiving, and were less prone to exhaustion, than those who helped out of a sense of duty. Interestingly, the partner being cared for also seemed to benefit: they were more satisfied with their relationship and, in some cases, felt greater pain relief.

Why would the internal motivations of helpers affect their partners? Sara Kindt, one of the coauthors of these studies, says it has to do with how motivation affects the caregivers' responsiveness toward their partner. "Autonomously motivated partners are more open, curious, and sincerely receptive to a partner's preferences and needs," she says. "In contrast, a partner's controlled helping motivation might be associated with reacting in a more restrictive, less responsive way."

That may be well and good, but isn't your motivation out of your control? It turns out it's not—at least not entirely. Instead, it might be possible to nudge it in a more autonomous direction with gratitude. In a recent study by Kindt and her colleagues, couples—where one member suffered from a painful condition called fibromyalgia and the other was a frequent caregiver—filled out daily questionnaires for two weeks. The caregivers reported on what motivated them to help their partners, whether they thought their partners were grateful, and to what degree helping kept them from fulfilling personal goals that day, like maintaining relationships with others, enjoying leisure time, working, or taking care of their own health.

Researchers found that on days when caregivers perceived more gratitude from their partners, their motivation to help was significantly more autonomous. It was less autonomous when they felt thwarted in fulfilling their goals—probably no surprise there. However, perceiving gratitude also had carryover effects, making caregivers more intrinsically motivated to help the next day, too. Conflicts with personal goals had no such carryover effects.

But giving thanks won't mean much if the receiver is closed to taking it in. While gratitude is hard to feel sometimes, it can also be hard to absorb. Kindt says it's important for people receiving thanks to recognize it and acknowledge it. Otherwise, they may miss out on a joyful, rewarding aspect of caring for another.

"Couples may benefit from expressing more gratitude, but also from learning to pay attention and to make positive attributions when spouses express gratitude to them," she says. In this case, a positive attribution means recognizing that a partner's thanks is an expression of their love and appreciation.

CHAPTER 15

How to Help Gratitude Grow in Your Kids
By Maryam Abdullah

A friend once vented about her teenage daughter being "so ungrateful!" She asked me, "How can she not know how much she has?" And this mom isn't alone. Parents hope (or even expect) that their children will grow up to be grateful. In a recent study, Amy Halberstadt and colleagues found that parents get peeved when their children don't show gratitude. As one parent said, "I can be embarrassed as a parent. I can feel angry at [my child] that he hasn't sufficiently conveyed gratitude when I thought he should."

How can parents set the stage for their children to be grateful? Research suggests that grateful parents raise grateful kids. One study by William Rothenberg, Andrea Hussong, and colleagues found that the more gratitude parents felt, the more often they set goals to foster gratitude in their six- to nine-year-old children. They also placed their children in more activities that provided opportunities for gratitude, such as family gratitude practices and social service events. And their kids expressed more gratitude.

These findings suggest that both parents' intentions and their actions are important for how gratitude develops in their children. As researchers Blaire Morgan and Liz Gulliford put it, "It is largely agreed that gratitude is not inbuilt; instead, it develops over time, as certain capacities become available and cognitive abilities mature." That is, cultivating gratitude takes patience.

What can parents do to help their children practice it? Here are some research-backed suggestions.

1. Help Young Children Understand Their Own and Others' Feelings and Thoughts

Although toddlers may learn to say thank-you, between preschool and kindergarten, they are likely still working on thinking about others' thoughts and feelings as separate and possibly different from their own. This understanding of others being separate from ourselves may be the foundation of expressing gratitude. As a parent, you'll be less frustrated when you align your expectations with your kids' cognitive development. Parents can be the scaffolds for their children's emerging gratefulness by giving them the language for the array of emotions and thoughts they and others may feel and think. It's always eye-opening to hear your young child's response to, "How do you think that person feels right now?"

2. Remind Older Children of the Adults in Their Lives That Are There for Them

Older children who feel that they can call upon their parents and teachers as sources of support tend to feel grateful. The gratitude may come from knowing that their parents or teachers are trustworthy, provide them with resources they need, or give them helpful feedback and advice. In addition to inspiring gratitude, positive relationships with close adults are critical for children's overall development. So, remind your older children to practice reflecting on their network of supportive grown-ups, on specific times of distress when these adults were sources of comfort and strength to them, and on how they felt upon receiving support.

3. Encourage Your Children to Participate in Gratitude-Rich Activities

Again, participating in gratitude-rich activities like family gratitude practices and volunteering can help kids develop gratitude. These activities provide children with occasions to think about others' circumstances more deeply and increase their awareness of their own good fortune and the gifts they've received from others. Witnessing how both peers and adults show gratitude when they participate in these types of activities—and how others respond to that gratitude—provides a model for how gratitude works. And kids may enjoy how their own actions fulfill others, which fulfills them, too.

In Halberstadt's study, parents shared that they wanted their children to be grateful for what they had, including shelter and food, but this can be a complicated feeling. The parents acknowledged some potential consequences when children recognize that not all people have those basic needs filled and that they, too, could lose them. Some parents believed that this realization could help children appreciate fully diverse human experiences; others felt that it would "challenge the innocence of childhood bliss." You may want to consider how to balance your gratitude goals for your children with your values and your children's development.

4. Take It One Day at a Time

Findings by Andrea Hussong and her colleagues suggest that parents can do a lot in day-to-day life to reinforce the importance of gratitude and teach kids to experience and express it. For example, perhaps you notice your child telling her grandparents how much it means to her that they cooked her favorite foods when she visited. In moments like this, you can tell your child how *you* feel about her expressing her gratitude to others or to you. You can also talk about why you feel thankful in moments of shared experience, such as appreciating the natural world when you are taking a hike together in the woods.

Such daily practices can become a pattern helping you model, teach, reinforce, and create opportunities to cultivate gratitude in your children. During dinner or immediately before bedtime, you and other family members can take turns sharing three good things that happened in your lives that day. With older children and teens, you can practice daily guided gratitude meditations together, which will help bring greater awareness of the many gifts in your kids' lives—from their bodies and possessions to beloved family and friends to modern technology and conveniences, such as electricity and running water, to institutions such as libraries and schools.

5. Expect Gratitude to Develop Bit by Bit

Gratitude may be experienced differently at different ages, as our understanding of gratitude matures with age. For adults, gratitude is often thought to involve feeling thankful or joyful for receiving a gift that was given to you voluntarily and intentionally by another. For children, gratitude may not involve all these adult experiences and expressions at the same time. Hussong and her team asked parents to look out for four different elements that can be part of children's gratitude: noticing they've received a gift; understanding that this gift was given to them on purpose by another; having positive feelings such as joy; and expressing their gratitude. Sometimes, children don't yet experience the link among all of these parts simultaneously. For example, a six-year-old may feel happy and thank her dad for a special beach picnic lunch on her birthday, but she may not yet fully connect her happiness to her dad's decision to take a day off work because he knows how much she loves sand castles and tide pools.

Taking this into account, parents can adjust their expectations about how their children experience gratitude, which will ward off disappointment when kids forget to say thank-you or don't seem to appreciate the sacrifices of others. It's better to notice your children's strengths—for example, the fact that they were delighted by a gift rather than feeling entitled to it. And from there, you can be your children's gratitude guide by helping them learn about the four parts of gratitude, and their possible connections, and by supporting your children wherever they are in their development.

6. Be Both Proactive and Reactive

Does parental guidance inspire children to be grateful, or do thank-yous from children prompt parents to talk about gratitude? Hussong's research isn't conclusive, but the answer is likely both. Nurturing gratitude can be a two-way street; parents and children can take turns leading the effort.

On the one hand, children who receive more encouragement from parents to develop gratitude may learn and show more gratitude and come to see that their parents value it. One way to offer this scaffolding is to make a point of expressing your own thanks in front of your children. When your partner goes out of the way to put gas in your car because you have a busy week ahead, talk about your gratitude over Sunday breakfast as a family.

On the other hand, children's spontaneous acts of gratitude may lead parents to pay more attention and set more goals to teach their children about gratitude. When you notice that your son is beaming with delight and hugs his aunt after she repairs his broken bicycle, ask him about his feelings, what it took for his aunt to fix his bike, why he thinks she chose to do so, and what kind of thank-you note or drawing he might create for her.

7. Communicate the Value of Gratitude to Your Children

In Halberstadt's study, some parents suggested that they had implicit expectations of their children when they gave them gifts, and they felt some resentment when their children did not express any gratitude.

One way to mitigate this is to have conversations with your children regularly about the importance you place on gratitude. Practice gratitude in front of your children and tell them how you feel when they express gratitude to you; engage children to think creatively about how they could express gratitude to others, and talk about others' positive responses to their efforts.

Spontaneous and unexpected expressions of gratitude from children are intensely moving to parents. They can make you hopeful that your kids feel deeply connected with others and that they'll strive to be compassionate in turn. But if you want to raise grateful kids, the key is to recognize that gratitude is a skill and to help them practice it just like any other.

CHAPTER 16

Feeling Entitled to a Little Gratitude on Mother's Day?

By Christine Carter

Here's an icky confession: Since becoming a mother, I have dreaded Mother's Day. The holiday has, somehow, left me feeling *un*appreciated. I've tended to get in a funk, and not out of grief or some sort of well-defined pain—I can only imagine how hard Mother's Day must be to someone who has lost their mother. I feel bad in a bratty way, like a toddler who is pissed that she's not getting what she wants. The worst version of myself has typically made her appearance, ironically, on the day that we were supposed to be celebrating my best, most beloved, self.

What is it that has left me so resentful on Mother's Day? What have I wanted so much that I haven't been getting? Until about an hour ago, I thought it was about gratitude. I wanted to be appreciated on Mother's Day in the way that we used to show appreciation to *my* mother. Research shows that when we express gratitude in our relationships, we become more attuned to our family members' efforts on our behalf. I was hoping for a little more attunement to all the work I do as a mom—mostly from my husband but also from the kids.

At least, the way I remember it (and my memory may be a little rosy), we'd bring my mom breakfast in bed, showering her with homemade cards and gifts. My dad would give my mom a funny card and a gift that he'd bought. We'd take a family bike ride on the path around St. Mary's College, with a picnic that my dad and I packed with help from the deli at Black's Market. Norman Rockwell could've painted us.

None of that actually seems hard to re-create, but for the love of God, my family has never even come close. Last year, I laid out my expectations clearly for my husband. "I'm fine with no gifts," I explained. "So long as there are cards and a *family activity*." This did not happen. With four active teenagers and a husband who refuses to plan anything more than a day in advance, our only family outings are planned by me.

For the record, three of the four children made me *beautiful*, heartfelt Mother's Day cards—Kelly-Corrigan-level cards. They were practically set to music, they were so thoughtful and moving. But that was not enough for me.

Expectations are a tricky thing. Unfulfilled, they set us up to ruin what is actually happening, as we ruminate over what we think ought to be happening. Painful thoughts—*How could he not do this for me, given all I do for this family? Does he not appreciate me at all?*—start to loop endlessly, triggering waves of disappointment.

So how could I make this year different? I had already lowered my expectations to no material gifts, and that didn't help me much; I was not sure I could lower them to *nothing*. In past years, I've made a massive effort to focus on myself less, by helping others, but ultimately, even that didn't really prevent me from feeling unappreciated myself. I felt entitled to a little gratitude, dammit. (Let's not miss the irony here: entitlement is pretty much the opposite of gratitude. And rarely do we attract the opposite of what we feel. Just as we don't foster other people's love by lashing out at them, my unbridled sense of entitlement wasn't exactly generating a mountain of appreciation.) Emotional traps like this—obsessing over my feelings of unmet expectations—are usually triggered by a mistaken belief. So where was the error in my thinking?

I really was feeling unappreciated by Mark, my husband. I felt like I sacrificed more for our family and children, and that he should recognize *and feel grateful for that.* I held a deep-seated conviction that *I gave more.* I spent more time doing the hardest parenting work, creating and enforcing structure and discipline, managing the near-constant drama of life with three teenage girls and an active adolescent boy.

Now, I should mention that, according to research, I am not alone in believing that I do more for our family than my husband does—but I might not be correct. When researchers add up the percentage of work each person in a couple says they do, they consistently find that the total ends up being more than 100 percent. So, if a mom says she does 65 percent of the household work, and her husband says he contributes a solid 50 percent, there is a 15 percent error in there somewhere—someone's miscalculating. Perhaps this was the heart of my mistaken belief?

My Mother's Day funk had grown out of my belief that I do and sacrifice more for our family than Mark does. And weirdly, I somehow thought that this seemingly massive imbalance could be righted through a Mother's Day display of profound appreciation. This is funny to me now, because clearly even the most magical Mother's Day outing would not dissolve my resentment. We needed to deal with its source.

"We need counseling," I announced to Mark. I sat down to work through what I wanted help resolving. What did I want Mark to do differently?

What I found, when I really thought hard about it, was that my assumptions about our division of labor were blatantly untrue. Believe me, I was *shocked* by this revelation. But it turned out that I had loads of evidence suggesting I *don't* do more for our family than Mark does. True, I do the bulk of the emotional labor. But he does nearly all the house and garden maintenance. We spend about the same amount of time in the car driving kids around. I plan our meals and cook; he shops and cleans up. We have a division of labor where he does the things he likes to do best (like mowing the lawn) while I get to do the things that I love to do (like talking to the kids about their feelings).

In truth, I am lucky to have a truly equal partnership. And I was harboring resentment out of habit rather than reality. At times, being a mother can feel so overwhelming; when the kids were little, I sometimes felt a little victimized by it all, a little trapped by the sheer magnitude of the way they'd taken over my life. My husband simply couldn't do many of the things that I was doing. Pregnancy, labor and delivery, and breastfeeding bred loads of occasions when only mama would do. My family could never repay me for the sacrifices I'd made for them, but they could, and *should*, show me a little gratitude for it. Hence my feelings of entitlement to a little Mother's Day appreciation.

Billy Collins wrote a poem about this. In it, Collins recounts the thousands of meals his mom cooked, and the good education she provided, and all the other zillions of things she did for him. In return, he gave her…a *lanyard* he made at camp. Collins concludes:

And here, I wish to say to her now,

is a smaller gift—not the worn truth

that you can never repay your mother,

but the rueful admission that when she took

the two-tone lanyard from my hand,

I was as sure as a boy could be

that this useless, worthless thing I wove

out of boredom would be enough to make us even.

Now, this is what I wish to tell my children and husband both: We are even, with or without lanyards and family outings on Mother's Day.

Because I am *not* trapped. I have not been victimized. There is no need for reparation. You don't owe me a darn thing, even gratitude. I don't *have* to do any of the many things I do for you or our family. I *choose* to do them. I do them because I love each of you so very much. Moreover, this love that I feel for you is the greatest gift I've ever been given. It is a great joy to be a mother in this family, our family. I'm deeply, profoundly grateful for all we are and all we have—together.

CHAPTER 17

What Being a Stepfather Taught Me About Gratitude

By Jeremy Adam Smith

I tried to raise my son to be grateful, but I never gave much thought to how parenthood might make me more grateful—or how gratitude might help me get through some of my toughest parenting challenges. To learn that, I had to become a stepfather.

I first met Alex when they were about eight years old. Back then, their mother—my partner, Michelle—called Alex her son. Shortly after turning thirteen, Alex informed us that they weren't a boy. They weren't a girl either; they described themselves as nonbinary.

It's taken a little while for Michelle, me, and my son—Alex's stepsibling—to wrap our heads around this change in identity and pronouns. But slowly and steadily, we're learning what it means to be transgender and nonbinary. Alex is teaching us. Alex has taught me a lot of things. Many of the lessons have been difficult ones.

It's always been easy for me to raise my son, Liko. He and I have moved through our respective stages of development in tandem with each other, riding a two-seat bicycle along the same path. As he has advanced through adolescence, Liko has become more like me, which helps me to see myself. And he differs from me in some important ways, differences I've had to learn to respect. In the years ahead, I can see our path splitting in two—and I'm learning to accept his independence. We always learn from people we take care of.

But Alex has challenged me in ways that Liko hasn't. Stepfathering is a task at which I fail every single week, one way or another. Most of the time, failure looks like me losing my temper. Sometimes, it's deeper than that.

Seeing my own son's good intentions is effortless, but there are times when I must fight with myself to see the best in my stepchild. Even though I know that when we lose hope for our children—when we fail to see their ability to grow—we catastrophically betray them.

This goes both ways, of course. My child has returned my optimism for him by idealizing me; my stepchild, on the other hand, seems to be constantly on the lookout for evidence of my faithlessness and ineptitude. To Alex, Michelle's moments of maternal rage seem to feel like tropical storms, unpleasant but natural—predictable, even. Michelle has had many crises of optimism for Alex—I've held her through some of them—yet all of us know that she would never, in the end, forsake her child. As for Alex's father's failures, those are easily forgotten, because we all train ourselves to live with our parents' shortcomings (though waking up to them, often in the teenage years, can be a merciless process for all concerned). My mistakes, on the other hand, loom large in Alex's imagination, as I've learned in family therapy sessions.

Over the years, I've realized that my failures are not wholly a product of my own individual weaknesses—which are many, to be sure—or of Alex's individual struggles, which are also many, but rather symptomatic of how freaking hard it is to be a stepparent and a stepchild. It doesn't matter, I think, how caring or successful or wise or present the stepparent is; the stepchild can love the stepfather with all their heart and still never feel at home with him in the same way they feel at home with their genetic father. Stepparents must meet much higher standards, as perhaps they should, if they want children to feel safe with them.

I have plenty of opportunities to screw up. We have primary custody, which means that I've spent a lot of time cooking for Alex and cleaning up after them and monitoring their chores and making sure they brush their teeth before bed. But, come Father's Day, I don't get a card from anyone acknowledging my place in Alex's life; there is never any appreciation or gratitude. How can there be? To honor me, the stepfather, would be to dishonor Alex's father. This feels normal, even to me.

A surprising amount of research suggests my experience is typical, if not universal. (There are always differences: I expect the age at which a child enters the stepparent's life is one of the biggest.) As psychologist Joshua Gold writes in *The Family Journal*, ambiguity and conflict and isolation all mark the experience of stepfathers, according to studies: "Boundary, role, and task confusion are seen as more prevalent in step than original, two-parent families due to the relative lack of formal models of stepfamily functioning." His language is passive and dry, in a way that belies the emotionally bloody work of forging a stepfamily.

I wasn't surprised to discover another research finding: stepfathers are often viewed by other family members as being much harder working than birth fathers. "Fathers may feel justified in being uninvolved with children as long as they are good providers," writes Gold. "However, in the case of stepchildren, such a notion does little to create a positive relationship." I certainly work harder as Alex's stepfather than I do as Liko's father. Almost every one of my interactions with Alex requires intention, self-control, questions, communication. With Alex, I risk disaster if I take anything for granted.

What can explain this discrepancy between the acknowledged hard work of stepfathers and the invisibility, and even hostility, they can suffer? Stepparents "are structurally vulnerable to being hated or resented, and there is precious little you can do about it, save endure, and commit to planting seeds of sanity and good spirit in the face of whatever shitstorms may come your way," writes Maggie Nelson in her splendid 2016 memoir, *The Argonauts*. "And don't expect to get any kudos from the culture, either: parents are Hallmark-sacrosanct, but stepparents are interlopers, self-servers, poachers, pollutants."

That's pretty much the problem in a nutshell. If the love between parent and child feels like the most natural and sacred thing in the world, then love between stepparent and stepchild can feel unnatural, and even wrong, to many people. So, why do it? Why would anyone ever take on the role of stepfather?

We become stepparents because we love the parent—and in helping raise Alex, I've gained a deeper, richer relationship with Alex's mother. Fatherhood didn't get any easier when I left my ex-wife; my nights with Michelle certainly didn't become more romantic when we moved in with each other's children. Our very worst fights have been over parenting. Both our previous marriages ended badly and, like many middle-aged divorced people, we entered our partnership feeling chastised and cautious. We know what breaks a home, and we haven't yet forgotten what it feels like to break. And so, when Michelle and I fight, we fight to understand, not to win. We accuse; we also forgive. We make mistakes; we apologize, too. Every conflict aims at resolution. Our voices rise, but our ears and hearts stay open, at least so far.

Through all these twists and turns, I have come to see my mate much more fully than I could have if we'd just stayed lovers and never tried to raise children together. I am witness to her incredible perseverance and her compassion when Alex is difficult. I see her weaknesses, too. In my own weak moments, her flaws can make me impatient. When I'm strong, they instead inspire tenderness in me. When I see her struggling as a mother, I try to struggle beside her. In trying to help her be stronger, I become stronger myself. None of this is easy, but it's not about easy or hard. It's about taking care of small humans until they get big enough to take care of themselves.

I often draw inspiration from the relationship between Michelle and her father, Jim. She calls him Dad, and he legally adopted her, but Jim came into Michelle's life as a prospective stepfather at roughly the same age I came into Alex's life. Michelle's birth father was not a good man. We like to believe that children are always better off with their natural-born parents, but sometimes the allegedly second-best stepparent is better, something I try to bear in mind when I feel inadequate.

From what I understand, at first, things were pretty tough between Jim and Michelle, especially in her teenage years. But today, they love each other, and they have a great relationship. Michelle is thriving, thanks in no small part to Jim, who did so much to help heal the damage caused by childhood abuse.

Which reminds me of what a long run parenthood can be. My interpretation of the facts, as I know them, is that Jim succeeded as a stepfather by simply being calm and steady and present. When things get rough with Alex, I try to be like Jim, or Jim as I imagine him to have been. Whatever my mistakes, however much I don't know, whenever I'm uncertain, I try to keep just showing up, and I try to never give up, and I try to keep learning what Alex has to teach me.

This process doesn't always lead to happiness—but it's not a child's job to make their parents happy. Alex gives me a much greater gift than happiness. They help give my life meaning.

I've alluded to my defeats as a stepfather, but there have been triumphs as well, even if they don't look terribly triumphant from the outside. Many times, I've been patient with Alex for just as long as I needed to be and then pushed them right when they needed that push—and I've felt the satisfaction of seeing them grow a little more. There have been moments when Alex has taken my hand as we walked down the sidewalk; I remember each one. I've felt pride when Alex designed a beautiful video game or played an original composition on their trumpet.

I felt wonder when I took Alex to the Multi-Specialty Transition Department at Kaiser and they faced a roomful of adults—me, a pediatrician, an endocrinologist, and an intern—to methodically explore what is involved with aligning their body with their inner sense of self. That was the moment when I really understood, in a concretely profound way, that Alex's transition wasn't "just a phase," but something they had to go through to become themselves. I learned something about Alex—how brave and determined they could be—and I learned quite a lot, on biological and spiritual levels, about our humanity.

It's through experiences like those that I've learned to love my stepchild. Love is inevitable when we nurture a life. However, life comes to us from different directions; that's why love must take different forms. I was there when my son came into the world, a double-footling breech. His tiny, bloody feet had never touched the Earth; they arrived without history. My stepchild came to me along another path, a stranger walking across the years alongside their mother. I've had to earn my place beside them; I have to earn it again every day. Most of the time, that means I just need to show up, however imperfectly, being there to help Alex in the horrendously wonderful hard work of growing up. My life matters more because of Alex. That's why I don't expect gratitude on Father's Day. It's Alex I thank for creating the opportunity to be their stepfather.

PART 5

How to Foster Gratefulness Around You

This part of the book tackles how to cultivate gratitude within organizations. At school and at work, you as an individual can't force other people to be more grateful. However, institutionally, we can create conditions that might encourage people to practice gratitude—which can in turn strengthen their relationships.

The following pages explore steps we can take to make gratitude more of a practice at schools and in the workplace; they combine pieces about research with more personal essays about the struggle to practice gratitude within larger groups. As Shawn Taylor describes in his essay, gratitude can feel more like a burden to those who are just trying to get through school and get good jobs.

That's why the evidence provided in this book is so necessary to support institutional change. Unfortunately, as research has shown, people can actually unlearn gratitude at school and at work, because saying or even hearing "thanks" makes them feel vulnerable. What can we do to change that? Read on.

CHAPTER 18

How to Foster Gratitude in Schools
By Jeffrey Froh and Giacomo Bono

In our research, we've tested concrete ways that educators can actually make youth more grateful—with very positive results. This research points to specific practices and principles that educators can weave into their classrooms. Perhaps the most commonly used technique for boosting gratitude—among adults and youth alike—is a gratitude journal.

In one early study, we asked middle-school students simply to list five things for which they were grateful, daily for two weeks, and we compared these students to others who were writing about hassles in their life or basic daily life events. Keeping a gratitude journal was related to more optimism and life satisfaction and to fewer physical complaints and negative emotions. Most significantly, compared to the other students, gratitude journalers reported more satisfaction with their school experience immediately after the two-week period, a result that held up even three weeks later.

This exercise is easy to implement. Regardless of the subject, educators can have students jot down what they are grateful for before class begins. To make the exercise more potent, students can describe why they are grateful for the things they list. Entries could even be posted on a gratitude wall as an artful reminder. We have solid scientific evidence that these practices boost students' moods, broaden their thinking, and energize greater learning.

Another exercise we've tested is the gratitude visit, in which students write a letter to someone who had helped them but whom they'd never properly thanked; the students read their letter in person to the recipient, then later discuss their experience with others who also completed a gratitude visit. When we conducted a study of the gratitude visit, we found that students who at the start were low in positive emotions reported more gratitude and positive emotions immediately after the study and greater positive emotions two months later, compared with students who didn't do a gratitude visit.

Building on this research, and research by colleagues, we have identified several key principles that educators can use to promote gratitude in their students—principles that we've incorporated into our own gratitude curriculum. This curriculum is intended to subtly instill grateful thinking in youth without requiring an explicit focus on gratitude. It emphasizes three key principles that can support a gratitude journal, a gratitude visit, or simply the practice of gratefulness in everyday life.

1. **Notice intentions.** Try to encourage students to appreciate the thought behind gifts they receive—to consider how someone noticed their need and acted on it. Our research suggests this goes a long way toward cultivating an attitude of gratitude among children and adults alike. For students in particular, knowing that others believe in them and their potential motivates self-improvement. To get them to reflect on the intentions behind the gifts they receive, teachers can ask, "Can you think of a time when a friend [or parent, teacher, or coach] noticed something you needed [for example, lunch] or remembered something you care about and then provided you with those things?" As students give examples, teachers could have them elaborate: "How did you know they helped you on purpose? How did you feel after they helped you?"

2. **Appreciate costs.** It's important to emphasize that when someone is helpful, that person usually sacrifices time or effort to provide the help. Teachers could ask, "What are some things your friend gave up to help you with that project?" Playground aides could say, "Wow, for your friend to come play

tag with you, he had to stop playing soccer, which I know is his favorite game." A librarian could point out, "How nice it was for that student to let you use their computer!"

3. **Recognize the value of benefits.** Teachers can also foster gratitude by reminding their students that when others help us, they are providing us with "gifts." This is one reason why, in our gratitude curriculum, we prompt students to focus on the personal value of the kind acts of others. Teachers can bring this up by having students complete the sentence stem "My day [or life] is better because…" and give examples, such as "…my teacher helped me when I didn't understand something" or "…my coach showed me how to be a better basketball player."

Studies of our gratitude curriculum have found that it can strengthen children's ability to think gratefully, and with this change comes improvement in their moods. A weekly version of the curriculum produced these effects up to five months later. A daily version had immediate effects (two days later) and led children to write 80 percent more thank-you cards to their PTA. Even their teachers found them happier. That this curriculum can be adapted to any program focused on kind, helpful, prosocial behavior makes it practical, too. What's more, we believe the benefits of gratitude can spread beyond students to teachers and staff, not only improving their work but helping to prevent burnout. This, in turn, can influence parents, providing common ground for investing in youth.

CHAPTER 19

Gratitude Is a Survival Skill
By Shawn Taylor

.

Growing up, I never had the chance to offer or reflect on gratitude. It was demanded of me, by force if necessary. If I forgot to say thank-you, or I was too slow with my thanks, a smack across the face or a belt to my behind served as a reminder. My mother wanted me to appreciate all the things she did for me.

The effect? I started to not ask for anything. I didn't ask for help on my homework. I didn't ask my mother to pass anything to me. I became hyper-self-sufficient. I was of the mind that if I asked for anything or forgot to be appropriately thankful, I would receive some kind of painful response.

I can confidently state that this is the reason why I did so poorly from kindergarten to sixth grade: I was deathly afraid if I asked my teachers for any kind of help, they would hurt me. I sometimes have fantasies about my childhood, my asking for help like my classmates did: Who would I be now? Would my dyslexia have been diagnosed earlier than it was? Would I have a better grasp on math? Would I be free of the nagging feeling that I'm not being thankful enough when people do something for me?

Later, in the early 1990s, I worked in a group home that was the stuff of nightmares. Violence, pain, and fear were the default settings of this place. There was a girl there—I'll call her Sunday. (I've changed all the kids' names in this piece.) She made four or five suicide attempts a week. Not self-harming gestures, but full-on attempts to take her life. Her story was so tragic as to be almost unbelievable: her father used her for sex as well as pimping her out to his drug-addled friends. Most of the people who hurt her were men. Despite this, she and I became close over our shared love of Britpop and science fiction.

When I quit that job to spend some time out of the country, I lost track of Sunday. In 2004, she called me. It took me a while to remember who she was—I'd worked with lots of youth over the years. She had a favor to ask. Sunday had completed college, had a job, and was about to get married. Since she didn't have any contact with her biological family, she asked if I would walk her down the aisle. It had been well over a decade since I'd worked with her, so I agreed—but I wanted to know, why me?

I was consistent, she told me. I listened to music with her and I gave her books: four photocopied pages at a time because the administrators of the group home thought she could harm herself with an entire book. I never gave up on her, Sunday said. This made her feel like she wasn't broken, that she mattered.

The wedding was beautiful. I've cried like that only two other times in my life: when I was married and when my daughter was born. At Sunday's wedding, I suddenly fully understood what gratitude was. With this invitation, she acknowledged the impact I'd had on her life. Not with a cursory thank-you, but with action. Her gratitude meant my presence in her life had value. Indeed, she valued me enough that she trusted me to bear witness to her new self. What I did for her, how I thought about her and interacted with her, had made a substantive difference. I'll never forget that.

Sunday also showed me that a mere thank-you is too easy. Now, if someone shows me kindness, does something for me that transforms me in any way, I try to do more than just say thank-you. I let them know what their actions mean to me and how I've been affected by them. I tell them I'm available and willing to return what they've shown me. Not as some kind of tit for tat, but to show my radical appreciation for their time and energy spent on me. Her expression of gratitude changed my life and forced me to see the difference between being courteous and thankful and being grateful.

Despite using the terms interchangeably, I see thanks and gratitude as different things. A "thanks" is about courtesy. It is acknowledging that someone has done something for you. I also feel like thankfulness is outwardly focused. I experience it as being transactional. Someone assists you, and your thanks is the receipt of that transaction. On the other hand, gratitude is simultaneously inwardly and outwardly focused. You appreciate what's been done to or for you, you appreciate the person or thing for providing you with the assistance or experience, and you recognize how they have made your life better, even if it is just for a moment.

We spend a whole lot of time talking about microaggressions—minute social slights steeped in bigotry and disregard—but we rarely (if ever) talk about microalliances: the joyful ways we come together over a mutually beneficial and transformative interaction, like an authentic expression of gratitude.

This is why, eventually, I left adolescent mental health and juvenile justice work: I found no gratitude in the work, no microalliances. At a certain point, I no longer felt effective or energized by the work. I was burned out, compassion-fatigued. Instead of being grateful that I was able to do this work, I became resentful. When the emotional return on investment is imbalanced, it is time to go.

I'm now the director of an alternative high school of choice. The program I run is for students who are behind in high school credits and won't be able to graduate "on time." Almost all are people of color, living at or below the poverty line. A large number identify as queer. Many are undocumented. It turns out that the skills I learned in my previous job working with teens with behavioral and mental health challenges, involved with the justice system, and just dealing with the persistent trauma of adolescence, come in handy. In fact, if I didn't have these skills, I'd never be able to do my job.

I think of the program as an Etch-A-Sketch: shake it up and begin from scratch. Starting fresh for these students isn't just about doing better in school but also about changing the way they view themselves, how they view the world, and how they view themselves in the world. The staff understands that when the students walk through our doors, they are walking into a new life.

Inviting students to make these changes is the most difficult part of the work. So many are beaten down by gentrification (we lose a handful of students each term because their families can no longer afford to live in Oakland or anywhere in the Bay Area), tragic loss, sexual violence, community despair. That they even come to school is a feat of resilience that I praise every chance I get. But this whole invitation to change is a process. And in this process, asking them questions, listening to their answers, and offering options (not advice) have proven to be valuable, especially when done in a group setting.

Three years in, my team and I have increased graduation rates, term-to-term persistence, and in-term retention. When I arrived, the program was considered a failure, but no longer. We became successful when I started treating the program less like a traditional school and more like a group home with a rigorous educational component. Check-ins with students, parental involvement, and more rewards than consequences helped transform the program from the last resort for students who didn't do well in traditional high school to a place where struggling students feel they can restart their stalled education.

I believe we were able to make these gains because of the premium placed on gratitude. Unlike in my house growing up—where gratitude was painfully extracted—I've tried to make gratitude a part of the cultural fabric of our school. It began simply with "please" and "thank you." Then it grew to random rewards for prosocial behaviors. It started with the staff but then grew beyond them, as students started to express more appreciation.

So many of our students are not used to this. Take Manny, for example. School wasn't Manny's thing. Never liked it. Before they graduated, they went to almost every high school Oakland had to offer. (Manny identifies as nonbinary, which is why I'm using "they" as a pronoun.) In Manny's admission interview, I reviewed their file with them and set some boundaries around previous behaviors that would be unacceptable at our school. I said that I trusted them enough to make safe decisions for themselves and those around them.

Manny had a rough first month, but at the end of every day with no behavioral problem, I expressed my thanks to them for choosing success over things that would hold them back. Manny accused me of insincerity and said, "You just want to make sure I don't whoop somebody's ass." I admitted that this was part of it. The other part, I stressed, was that I was genuinely grateful they were making decisions to change their behavior for the better. When I told them they did well, it made me feel good, and that gave me energy that I could invest in making the program the best it could be for them and their fellow students. "Thank you for making me want to come to work every day," I told them. Manny eventually graduated with a 3.5 grade point average—up from 0.34— and they are now attending a four-year college.

I work with students like Manny one on one, but I also work with students in groups. These groups almost always bring about shifts in perspective, if even a tiny bit, but I had a group earlier this year that—I won't say it broke my heart, but I will say it challenged me to recommit to this population because of the sadness I felt.

When the group was scheduled to begin, I sat alone in the circle of chairs as the nineteen high schoolers milled about. I made eye contact with some, avoided eye contact with others, but remained silent until they began to fill the remaining seats. I always stay quiet like this, listening to the scattered conversations, and waiting patiently until they are ready to begin. It is their time, and I let them have some control over it. In this group, we've talked about everything from body integrity and sovereignty to media representations of race and gender to why I've never smoked, drunk, or done any drugs in my life. Nothing is off topic, as long as it is explored with respect and compassion. A year earlier, many students in the group had experienced the loss—to murder—of one of their classmates. We were right around the anniversary of this death, so I decided to introduce what I thought would be a light topic. "What are you thankful for?" I asked the group.

It was like I had told a horrible joke, to the wrong crowd, in the wrong room. Complete silence. Even students who always contributed stayed quiet. I'm normally really good with silence, but this silence didn't feel right. I dropped a few more prompts, but nothing. I rephrased the question—still nothing. One of the students began to offer things she liked. I grabbed on to this thread and tried to shoehorn it into a conversation about gratitude. It didn't work. Another student became upset and launched into, "Thankful for what? For being poor, my brother in jail, my mom working all kinds of jobs?" I validated the student, then pressed, "You're here. You're trying to change your life, right?" He countered, "Why would I be thankful for something I'm doing to better myself? Ain't nobody helping me." Many of the students nodded or murmured in agreement.

I felt so sad and defeated. The words stung because of their familiarity. I understood why the student felt that way and why the others agreed. The world, their world, is a hard place to live. When everything appears to be conspiring to impede your progress, then despair, resentment, and retaliation seem to be the only options. I could empathize. I was also ashamed of how easy it was for me to do so. My trauma is still pretty close to the surface. How could I get it so right with my staff but so damn wrong with my students? And if these students couldn't express gratitude, what kind of lives would they live? Gratitude relates to kindness and a mutuality of kindness, and this was something my students lacked: kindness done to them and the ability to be kind without conditions. And I don't blame them. They live in worlds where the "I" is the most important thing—where getting yours is the only way they can get anything. This didn't make it any less sad and painful.

After several more minutes of profoundly awkward silence, we adjourned and I went to my office to call some staff members together to process what had just happened. I think this experience affected me so deeply because I was forced to realize how gratitude, no matter how hard I'm working on it, still isn't my strong suit. I try, but I fall short more than I like. I saw my younger self in all of them.

This attitude of gratitude was something that I've wanted my daughter to never have to unlearn. I didn't want her youth to be as miserable as mine. From a young age, gratitude has been a factor in my daughter's life. After she was born, my wife and I modeled "please" and "thank you." When she was older, we'd sing, "You get what you get, and you don't throw a fit," to invite her to be appreciative of what she had and who spent time with her. If she forgot, we'd have a conversation with her about why.

At age ten, she has such a developed and nuanced expression of gratitude that I learn from her every day. Most mornings we set a goal or two for the day. When we see each other in the evenings, we discuss if she achieved her goals. If so, we talk about what she did to make it happen. If not, we discuss barriers and ways she can take different actions to get her desired result. She also has a gratitude jar on her desk. She writes down what she's grateful for and puts it in the jar. At the end of the week, she opens the jar and reflects on all the things she was grateful for.

My daughter has two parents, and we're raising her in an emotionally and financially stable household of relative privilege. How many marginalized and disproportionately impacted people are getting lessons like those she's receiving, being trained in gratitude from an early age? But I don't see gratitude as a luxury. I see gratitude as a survival skill. The ability to appreciate and to recognize the good and to be thankful for it helps heave off the weight of the things that are determined to hold us back, to hold us down.

So, I keep trying to be kind to my students—as a model to them for what gratitude means, the way Sunday was a model to me—and to teach them to be kind in turn: even on the days that this feels impossible, like it did with the students in group that day. Being able to look at the world from a place of interconnectedness is powerful. Knowing that your actions and words mean something to someone, that you matter to someone—as Sunday expressed to me—instills a perspective, a momentum, that invites us to participate in the world in a way that emphasizes cooperation and connection. It allows us to reenvision ourselves, reenvision the world, and reenvision our relationship with the world. To use a very clichéd phrase, we're all we got.

CHAPTER 20

Five Ways to Cultivate Gratitude at Work

By Jeremy Adam Smith and Kira Newman

According to a 2013 survey of two thousand Americans by the John Templeton Foundation, people are less likely to feel or express gratitude at work than anyplace else. And they're not thankful for their current jobs, ranking their jobs dead last in a list of things they're grateful for. It's not that people don't crave gratitude at work, both giving *and* receiving. Ninety-three percent agreed that grateful bosses are more likely to succeed, and only 18 percent thought that gratitude made bosses "weak." Most reported that hearing "thank you" at work made them feel good and motivated.

But here comes the messed-up, mysterious, and interesting part: almost all respondents reported that saying thank-you to colleagues "makes me feel happier and more fulfilled," but on any given day, only 10 percent acted on that impulse. A stunning 60 percent said they "either never express gratitude at work or do so perhaps once a year." In short, Americans actively suppress gratitude on the job, even to the point of robbing themselves of happiness.

Why? It may be because, in theory, no one gives away anything at work; every exchange is fundamentally contractual and economic. You don't deliver that memo to your boss at three o'clock sharp out of the goodness of your heart, but because that is what you're being paid to do, because that's what's in your job description. Your thanks is a paycheck. Fail to do what you're asked, and you may not see another one.

"We tend to think of organizations as transactional places where you're supposed to be 'professional,'" says Ryan Fehr, a professor of management at the University of Washington in Seattle. "We may think that it's unprofessional to bring things like forgiveness or gratitude or compassion into the workplace."

Tellingly, only those who earned $150,000 or more were likely to express any gratitude for their jobs, according to the Templeton survey. This hints at one of the factors that undermines gratitude at work: power and pay imbalances. What's more, in a 2012 study, M. Ena Inesi and colleagues found that people with power tended to believe others thanked them mainly to win favor, not out of authentic feeling—and as a result of this cynicism, supervisors are themselves less likely to express gratitude.

Indeed, the Templeton survey found that 35 percent of respondents believed that expressing any gratitude could lead coworkers to take advantage of them. When we acknowledge our interdependency, we make ourselves vulnerable. (And in fact, gratitude is not always the best response, even when good things have happened to you, in situations of fundamental inequality—see Amie Gordon's essay, "Five Ways Giving Thanks Can Backfire," in part 3.)

The result is a vicious, culturally ingrained circle of ingratitude, which can have a terrible effect on workplace morale and cohesion. Why should this be the case? Because the need for a paycheck is only one of the motivations we bring to work. We don't just work for money. We also work for respect, for a sense of accomplishment, for a feeling of purpose. We invest ourselves and our emotions into our jobs, and work affects our emotional states.

Gratitude is a nonmonetary way to support those nonmonetary motivations. Even a simple thank-you helps; it doesn't cost a dime, and it has measurably beneficial effects. In a series of four experiments, psychologists Adam Grant and Francesca Gino found that receiving a thank-you from a supervisor gave people a strong sense of both self-worth and self-efficacy. Grant and Gino's study also reveals that the expression of gratitude has a spillover effect: when gratitude is regularly expressed, people become more trusting of each other and more likely to help each other out.

The benefits of gratitude go beyond a sense of self-worth, self-efficacy, and trust between employees. When Greater Good Science Center gratitude project codirector Emiliana Simon-Thomas analyzed data from our interactive journal, Thnx4.org, she found that the greater the number of gratitude experiences people had on a given day, the better they felt overall. People who kept at it for at least two weeks showed significantly increased happiness, greater satisfaction with life, and higher resilience to stress; this group even reported fewer headaches and illnesses. Building a culture of gratitude at work is not easy, but the science says it's worth it. Here are five research-tested tips for fostering gratitude in the workplace.

Start at the Top

Employees need to hear thank-you from the boss first. This is one of the clearest takeaways from research into workplace gratitude. It needs to start at the top because expressing gratitude can make some people feel unsafe, particularly in a workplace with a history of ingratitude. It's up to the people with power to clearly, consistently, and authentically say thank-you in both public and private settings, to establish this as a company norm.

These efforts can also translate into protocols and procedures. When hiring someone new, bosses can ask, "How do you wish to be thanked?" When an employee leaves, throw them a good-bye party and take a moment to express appreciation for their qualities and contributions. Gratitude can also be built into performance reviews and staff meetings, where five minutes can be allocated for people to say thanks to each other for all they do.

Southwest Airlines used to send out pins to employees who had served the airline for a milestone number of years (like five or ten). To better honor their culture of appreciation, though, the airline now sends the pins to leaders and invites them to recognize and celebrate employees in a special way, transforming gratitude from a faceless gift into a relationship-building experience. Inviting leaders to participate communicates to everyone that gratitude and well-being are important.

Thank the People Who Never Get Thanked

Every organization has a class of employee that hogs all the glory. In hospitals, it's doctors. At universities, it's faculty. And every organization has high-profile people. But what about those who cut the checks, submit the invoices, mop the floors, write the copy? Thanking those who do thankless work is crucial because it provides the foundation for gratitude at every level of the organization. Yes, at a university, faculty do the research and teaching that's core to the school's mission. But without a cadre of staff behind them, they'd have to raise money for their own salaries and empty their own wastebaskets. Public appreciation of administration and physical staff makes their contributions visible and thus broadens everyone's understanding of how the organization functions—and needless to say, it improves morale and increases trust.

For Ryan Fehr at the University of Washington, one of the keys to a successful gratitude initiative is consistency. "Ultimately, it's about creating an organizational culture around gratitude," says Fehr. "Organizations need to, as a baseline, treat their employees well, and then, on top of that, the organization needs to develop programs that help them see all of these positives."

"Acknowledging the thoughts and efforts of people with gratitude shows that those people matter," says consultant Stephanie Pollack. "When I've seen it work, it's just life changing."

Aim for Quality, Not Quantity

Forcing people to be grateful doesn't work. It feeds the power imbalances that undermine gratitude in the first place, and it can make expressions of gratitude feel inauthentic. The key is to create times and spaces that foster voluntary, spontaneous expressions of gratitude. It's also the case that studies show there is such a thing as too much gratitude—it seems trying to be grateful every day induces gratitude fatigue.

How do you convey authenticity? Details are decisive. When you are specific about the benefits of a person, action, or thing, it increases your own appreciation—and it tells someone that you are paying attention rather than just going through the motions.

We should also think about *how* individuals like to be thanked. Pollack likens appreciation to love languages: each individual's language of appreciation is different, and we risk miscommunication if we assume everyone likes to receive a card, a coffee, or public praise. Workplaces can bring together diverse people with different types of communication styles, backgrounds, and expertise, and it's our job to recognize our colleagues' strengths even if those strengths are different from our own.

"The key is that there are things to learn from each other," Pollack says. "Instead of being frustrated, it's celebrating that *Oh that person actually is seeing something I wouldn't see in the same way*. So, we can learn how to appreciate that."

Provide Many Opportunities for Gratitude

When people are thanked for their work, they are more likely to increase their helping behavior and provide help to others. But again, not everyone likes to be thanked—or likes to say thank-you—in public. They may be shy or genuinely modest. The key is to create many different kinds of opportunities for gratitude. Can an office keep a gratitude journal? Of course! The administration and finance office at the University of California, Berkeley, created an appreciation platform that allows employees to recognize each other's contributions, which feeds into a Kudos web page that publicly highlights these contributions. You don't need to build a website—a bulletin board, sometimes called a "gratitude wall," will do. But this kind of project will work best if it encourages the thank-you to target actual human beings instead of things. We are all thankful for coffee, for example, but the gratitude should go to Mary, the administrative assistant who makes the coffee every morning.

Gift giving is another way to foster gratitude. Research shows that giving gifts may have an important effect on working relationships and reciprocity—and nonmonetary gifts are the most beneficial of all. Giving creates gratitude, but giving can also be a good way to express gratitude, especially if the person in question is shy. You can say thank-you by taking on scut work, lending a parking space, or giving a day off. These kinds of nonmonetary gifts can lead to more trust in working relationships—provided it's reciprocal, sincere, and altruistically motivated.

There is one more (albeit tricky) way of fostering gratitude: research points to the notion that gratitude might have positive effects on transforming conflicts, which can benefit the organization and working relationships. How do you do that? It starts with the person charged with mediating the conflict: a supervisor with two bickering employees might open a meeting by expressing sincere appreciation of both parties. Throughout the process, that person should never miss an opportunity to say thank-you. The research says this attitude of gratitude will have a positive feedback effect, even if results aren't obvious right away.

In the Wake of Crisis, Take Time for Thanksgiving

Cultivating a culture of gratitude might be the best way to help a workplace prepare for stresses that come with change, conflict, and failure. Making gratitude a policy and a practice "builds up a sort of psychological immune system that can cushion us when we fall," as Robert Emmons writes in chapter 13. "There is scientific evidence that grateful people are more resilient to stress, whether minor everyday hassles or major personal upheavals."

Gratitude helps employees see beyond one disaster and recognize their gains. Ideally, it gives them a tool to reframe a loss as a potential gain. If your office has gone through a crisis, hold a meeting with the aim of gaining a new perspective on the incident. Emmons proposes a series of questions to help people recover from difficult experiences, which we've adapted here for the workplace:

- *What lessons did the experience teach us?*

- *Can we find ways to be thankful for what happened to us now, even though we were not at the time it happened?*

- *What ability did the experience draw out of us that surprised us?*

- *Are there ways we have become a better workplace because of it?*

- *Has the experience removed an obstacle that previously prevented us from feeling grateful?*

The science says we Americans need to overcome our aversion to gratitude on the job and see it instead as just one more career skill we can cultivate alongside others like communication, negotiation, and forgiveness. It's something anyone can learn—from which everyone will benefit.

What Does a Grateful Organization Look Like?

By Emily Nauman

The Greater Good Science Center, in consultation with researchers from the Expanding the Science and Practice of Gratitude project and Kim Cameron of the Center for Positive Organizational Scholarship at the University of Michigan Ross School of Business, has developed a quiz that measures the level of gratitude in an organization. The quiz asks people how much gratitude they see around them in their organization, from the highest levels on down, and how much gratitude they themselves have received there.

When we analyzed six hundred responses, we found that about 30 percent said they were from outside of the United States; the rest were scattered across the country, with the biggest representation from the West Coast and the Midwest. Also, though the respondents hailed from diverse organizations, nearly half worked in a for-profit business office. Here's what we learned about how *Greater Good* readers see and experience gratitude in their organizations.

The type of organization predicted how much gratitude people perceive there. Though many organizations had similar levels of gratitude, community service organizations had the highest—significantly greater than businesses, health care providers, and governmental agencies (the latter two had the lowest scores). "This result is consistent with other findings showing that the opportunity to make a meaningful contribution is associated with elevated gratitude," notes Kim Cameron in an email commenting on the results. "Contribution trumps receipt of rewards."

Position in the company matters. Those in high-level positions reported that they perceived more gratitude in their organization than those in low-level positions. Interestingly, the perception of gratitude in an organization declined with age unless the respondent was in a high-level position or an executive of the organization. This finding may indicate that high-level employees and executives are more likely to be thanked and to thank others, whereas folks lower on the ladder are more likely to be taken for granted, especially as they get older. Young people in low-level positions may hope to be promoted and eventually become a significant contributor, Cameron speculates. As people age, they may realize that the possibility to advance is no longer likely, and their perception of their organization declines as a result.

Stress level predicted gratitude. Organizations high in stress tended to be low in gratitude. Organizations with more than fifty people were also lower in gratitude than smaller organizations, but this effect disappeared when controlling for stress. In other words, large organizations tended to be more stressful environments, which was why they were low in gratitude. It seems likely that environments high in stress are also environments with tight deadlines, so feeling like they're short on time could hinder people from pausing to express gratitude. On the other hand, the effect could run in the opposite direction: less gratitude could lead to more stress. People with high volumes of work may have a harder time coping if they feel that their hard work goes unrecognized.

Gratitude as a Pathway to Positive Emotions at Work

By Kira Newman

Gratitude isn't the only emotional skill that could be valuable to the modern business. We might also hope to build emotionally intelligent and empathic workplaces, where employees practice compassion and forgiveness. But gratitude could be a pathway to these (arguably more difficult) goals, according to Peter Bonanno, director of program development at the Search Inside Yourself Leadership Institute (SIYLI), a nonprofit that offers training in mindfulness and emotional intelligence to individuals and teams. Bonanno has found that, to most people, practicing gratitude is appealing, practical, feel-good, and fun. One study, for example, found that gratitude journaling for as little as fifteen minutes was enough to boost positive emotions.

What's more, being grateful to someone who has helped you means that you recognize the intentions and effort behind their actions, which is good practice for the "putting yourself in someone else's shoes" involved in empathy. "I see gratitude as a gateway drug to empathy in that it's very positive, and it's easy to get started with," Bonanno says.

At SIYLI retreats, Bonanno often leads a ten-minute gratitude meditation. Participants think of someone they want to appreciate, then focus on how they were impacted by that person and what their gratitude feels like. Afterward, they're invited to send the person a text message expressing their thanks. "It's a total heart opener," says Bonanno. "A lot of people have said that it's helped them open up a conversation that they've needed to have with a business partner or a spouse, something they've been holding in, something they've been putting off."

In another workshop, Bonanno saw the power of gratitude to promote kindness and generosity at work. Some participants from a large technology company reported experiencing feelings of guilt during a gratitude practice. Focusing on the good in their lives made them recognize all their privileges—enviable jobs, fun benefits, high salaries. After sharing and discussing these feelings, they left the workshop vowing to find ways to give back to people who were less fortunate.

That's an outcome you might expect from practicing gratitude. Studies show that grateful employees are more concerned about social responsibility, for example, probably because gratitude strengthens relationships and helps us see people's otherwise invisible contributions. Grateful employees—as well as employees who receive more gratitude—also perform more *organizational citizenship* behaviors, kind acts that aren't part of their job description, like welcoming new employees and filling in for coworkers. In fact, gratitude and kindness seem to form a positive loop in the workplace—just as they do inside the human brain, as other essays in this book describe.

CHAPTER 21

Why Health Professionals Should Cultivate Gratitude

By Leif Hass

Even at ninety years old and eighty-four pounds, Ms. Z had quite a presence. As her doctor, I admired the quiet strength she packed into her tiny frame. I wasn't surprised to hear that she had lived independently until recently, when she was hospitalized with shortness of breath—a residual effect of the tuberculosis she had contracted in her youth.

In the hospital, Ms. Z's breathing had improved, but not her strength, and it became clear that she would need more care upon her release. Working together, the family and I came up with a plan to keep her out of a nursing home. I was a little worn out from all the logistics. "Great, we have a plan to get you home," I said as I left her hospital room. "Good luck—and thanks."

In the hallway, I stopped and took a deep breath. It started to sink in how challenging it was going to be for her family to provide 24/7 care for Ms. Z—and also what a privilege it had been for me to care for her, to witness her family's devotion, to ease her suffering, to imagine the course of her life as it neared its end, and to fulfill her dying wish to go home. I reentered her room and saw Ms. Z sleeping, her kids conferring around a stack of bills. I took a deep breath.

"I wanted to let you know that I think you have a beautiful family," I said. "Your efforts to help your mom are inspiring. I want to thank you for letting me play a role in caring for her."

As I walked toward the door, I felt a visceral surge of emotion in my chest that rose to my head. Off balance and with tears coming to my eyes, I stood and wondered what brought on these intense yet wonderful sensations.

Why had these two, separate thank-yous to the same family provoked such different reactions in me? I found an answer to that question when I learned more about research on gratitude. This research clearly suggests that gratitude carries important benefits to mental and physical health: it boosts our mood and satisfaction with life; there's even evidence linking it to improved cardiovascular health among people at risk for heart disease. But for me, the research also helps explain what constitutes an effective expression of gratitude, one that makes it more likely that we'll enjoy those positive benefits. And I believe that these authentic experiences of gratitude can revitalize the work of health professionals like myself—at a time when many of us need the help.

The Need for Gratitude in Health Care

I work as a hospitalist—that is, a family practice doc who works exclusively with those in the hospital. This has allowed me to see up close the epidemic of burnout afflicting so many of my colleagues. Nearly 40 percent of physicians are affected by burnout, meaning that they feel physically and mentally exhausted, become less able to connect with their patients, and lose the ability to find meaning in their work. The technical, emotional, and time demands of the work can easily render care providers unhappy and unable to provide the empathic care their patients need. I have come to believe that developing and expressing strong feelings of gratitude for the good that does exist is one possible solution to this problem. My experience with the Z family crystallized this for me.

As a younger doctor, I thought thank-yous delivered at work were simply a forced, impersonal customer-service tool—the kind of "emotional labor" described by sociologist Arlie Hochschild in her book *The Managed Heart*. After ten years of medical practice, though, I realized that I needed to do more to support my patients emotionally during their time in the hospital. I thought familiar and reassuring language might comfort my elderly patients. So, despite my reservations, I started thanking my patients with the hope that they would feel comforted by the exchange.

In fact, I found that these thank-yous not only supported my patients but also gave me an immediate burst of energy and renewed passion for my work. Both my patients and I felt good after these short conversations, but for quite a while I didn't take the time to understand why this was, and what made for a truly effective thank-you. Once I did, however, the revelation was game changing for me and my work. The key for me lies in how Robert Emmons defines gratitude in the first chapter of this book: as a recognition of the gifts that others give us, a recognition of the source of those gifts, and an appreciation of those gifts. That experience can often lead grateful people to "pay it forward."

In a well-known study led by Emmons, people who kept a journal of things for which they were grateful enjoyed a more sustained sense of well-being in their lives and became more motivated to help others. In the health care setting, however, understanding this cycle can be tricky and a little counterintuitive. Who is doing the giving? And exactly what are the gifts?

Recognizing Gifts

When I mention gratitude to my colleagues, I often hear, "I sure wish that more of my patients were grateful for all I do." We are giving meds and advice and, at times, saving lives, so, as care providers, we can easily get caught up in all we are doing—and fail to see that the real story is the patient's life, and thus we miss the gift that is the beauty of the lives before us.

Crises from serious illness provoke existential struggles among patients and their families. Witnessing families navigate these struggles firsthand is as rich an experience as life offers; being able to heal in this setting transforms a rich experience into a profound privilege and a gift. These gifts can be missed if we don't take the time to recognize them.

The source of these gifts lies in the openness and trust of the patients who let us into their lives. I have learned to see a beautiful story in almost every room I enter: the love between an elderly couple, the unflinching care and support of a devoted daughter, the faith and optimism in those facing a grave diagnosis. With each visit, I am afforded an intimate view into fundamentally human emotions and struggles. That is a precious gift indeed.

But to appreciate the gifts we are given as care providers, we need to receive them properly. I try to slow down before each encounter with a patient, often with a deep breath, so that I will have the presence of mind to see the beauty in my patients' struggles. With intentionality, I thank them for letting me be involved in their lives at this important time. I also try to say an affirmation prior to clinic or rounds, such as this one we developed with the chaplaincy at my hospital: "Let us take a moment to acknowledge the suffering of those under our care and acknowledge all the love and hard work we give each day to each other and our patients."

Appreciating the Gifts

Time demands and high-stakes situations mean that many health care professionals are running all day. A moment to slow down with deep breaths and reflect, which I took before the second time I thanked the Z family, can do more than prepare us mentally for gratitude; it can prepare us physiologically. Research has found that deep breaths calm the stress-driven sympathetic nervous system and activate the para-sympathetic nervous system, which helps us bond with others, partly thanks to the hormone oxytocin. With a calmed nervous system, I could recognize and appreciate the gifts the family had given me, opening me up to a wave of gratitude and a parasympathetic-oxytocin system rush, which left me in tears.

By taking time to make ourselves mentally and physiologically receptive, as health providers, we can experience gratitude more profoundly. We can help our colleagues appreciate the gifts, too, by being gratitude leaders. This means thanking and acknowledging teammates for their compassion and care throughout the day. Along those lines, I try to acknowledge those who have contributed to my own success, identifying the specific gifts they gave me.

Paying It Forward

Burnout is characterized by emotional exhaustion, depersonalization, and a reduced sense of personal accomplishment, and I'll admit that I've been in that downward spiral before. What gratitude offers is a positive cycle. In one study, health care providers who twice weekly wrote down things for which they were grateful reported less stress and depression. Those who wrote down things that bothered them at work only became more frustrated. What's more, upon receiving a gift, people often feel a surge of positive emotion and a desire to give back, which can motivate us to pay it forward, by helping someone else. Feelings of gratitude make us more likely to help a stranger.

As it turned out, I would need that ability to pay it forward just moments after leaving Ms. Z's room for the second time. My next patient, Mr. J, was just across the hall, and I could see his son pacing in the room with evident frustration. Mr. J had come in the night before with pneumonia; overnight, he became more short of breath, then so confused and combative that we had to restrain him and give him a little medication to calm down. With his father weak and unresponsive, wrists tied to the bed the next day, Mr. J's son had reason to be confused and angry.

Because I felt uplifted from my experience with the Z family, I had the patience to empathically listen to the son's frustrations and concerns. If I had walked into that room feeling stressed, as I had felt after the first thank-you, I could have potentially clashed with him, saying something stupid in frustration like, "You think you're having a bad day? Well, I still have dozens of patients to see and am going to be way late driving the soccer car pool!" Best-case scenario, I would have barely been able to suppress my frustration, then finished my workday feeling burned out. Mr. J and his son—and the rest of my patients— would have been denied the best care possible.

Since that day with the Z family, I have been struck repeatedly by the power of gratitude. Understanding how gratitude works has transformed the way I experience my work as a health care provider. Now, if I have not teared up by the end of a shift, I wonder what gifts I missed that day. Contrary to what some may think, I believe this has only made me a stronger care provider, not a weaker one.

How One Provider Is Fostering Gratitude in Health Care

By Catherine Brozena

In San Diego, California, Scripps Health has taken steps to generate widespread commitment to a culture of gratitude all year round. The regional health system encompasses four hospitals across five campuses and a network of outpatient centers and clinics. While it is on the smaller side, with three thousand affiliated physicians and fifteen thousand employees, Scripps has shown what it can look like to hard-wire gratitude across the operations of a health care system.

The organization uses an online recognition platform for sharing expressions of gratitude between staff and leadership. The platform, called Excel Together, enables users to send notes of appreciation, makes it easy to recognize caregivers who do their jobs well through an electronic "wall of fame," and incentivizes gratitude through a system of points that staff can redeem for gifts and benefits. While the platform is largely designed for the workforce, patients are also able to express gratitude for the care they receive in the form of handwritten cards that are inputted into the system.

Paul Randolph, the director of Scripps's employee assistance program, says Scripps Health tries to capture gratitude in its online system even when that gratitude is expressed on the go. "Our staff providing patient care may not get on a computer easily," he says. "So there are cards on patient floors, and staff use these readily to handwrite their gratitude. These then become incorporated into staff huddles and meetings and are fed into the electronic system."

Scripps's comprehensive approach to fostering a culture of gratitude also takes the form of professional development programs that teach the importance of building gratitude into leadership and management styles and includes bulletin boards throughout its medical facilities where patients or staff can publicly post their gratitude to Scripps employees. "Part of the success in cultivating gratitude is making it routine for people to share their appreciation for each other's efforts in real time so that it becomes part of the culture," says Randolph.

CHAPTER 22

How to Help Other People Become More Grateful
By Tom Gilovich

Most people want to be grateful. Most people would rather be full of gratitude than feel entitled or resentful. But as we all know, gratitude can be elusive, and feelings of resentment and entitlement have a way of creeping in.

Much of the excellent gratitude research conducted over the past twenty years has therefore focused on what people can do to experience more of this healthy, productive emotion. That is, most research on gratitude is aimed at trying to promote it. But as Kurt Lewin, the father of social psychology, emphasized many years ago, there is a limit to how much change any of us can bring about when we try to motivate people who are already highly motivated. For example, people with difficulty breathing might be highly motivated to stop smoking, but they don't, because the habit is stronger than the motivation to quit. The better approach in these situations, he noted, is to figure out what's preventing the person from acting and then try to eliminate those barriers. In the field of gratitude research, are there further gains to be made by focusing on what prevents people from feeling grateful?

I believe there are, and my students and I have been conducting research aimed at understanding the *enemies of gratitude*. What have we found? Enemy number one is easy to identify: adaptation. Simply put, we all get used to things over time and start to take them for granted. But my research has also uncovered ways that we as individuals—and hopefully even societies—can start to overcome this barrier.

How to Make Gratitude Last

People have a remarkable capacity to adapt to anything that comes their way. That capacity is a great resource when we experience something negative. It's what allows us to recover from trauma and get over setbacks that make it seem like life "will never be the same." Adaptation can't make things literally the way they were, but it can make us feel as good and as fulfilled as we were beforehand.

Although adaptation can be a great resource when it comes to overcoming negative events, it is a powerful enemy when it comes to continuing to enjoy positive events. We think that things will be different when we get that job offer, that promotion, or that longed-for reciprocation of romantic interest. And things are different, but generally only for a while. These improvements in our lives become the new baseline to which we adapt, and we soon need something more to provide the same level of satisfaction, excitement, or joy.

What to do about this formidable enemy of happiness? People do not adapt equally to everything, and so it's useful to consider what sorts of things they adapt to less easily. That's what we did when we examined the gratitude people feel for the purchases they've made. My research team and I decided to investigate whether people feel more (and more enduring) gratitude for their material purchases—a bookcase, a jacket, or a piece of jewelry—or their experiential purchases, such as tickets to see a favorite band in concert, lessons from a respected coach or teacher, or travel to a far-off land dreamt about since childhood.

In the simplest test of this idea, we asked survey respondents to think about either a recent material purchase that cost more than a hundred dollars or a recent experiential purchase that cost that much. They then rated how happy they were with the purchase and how grateful it made them. The respondents felt significantly more grateful for the experiences they had purchased—they seemed to be less adapted to them.

Additional evidence comes from an analysis of online purchase reviews. We downloaded a total of 1,200 reviews from websites devoted to material products (CNET, Amazon) and to experiences (Yelp, TripAdvisor) and then had raters (who were unaware of the purpose of our investigation) rate each review for how much it conveyed a feeling of gratitude about the purchase. There were significantly more expressions of gratitude in the reviews posted on the experience-oriented websites.

Finally, gratitude researchers have shown that being grateful makes it easier for people to get in touch with their best self, and this is reflected in a willingness to move beyond selfish impulses and give to others. So, we decided to test whether experiential purchases would also spur more generosity than material purchases.

We had people reflect on the most significant material or experiential purchase they had made in the past five years. Then, participants played a laboratory game in which they decided how much of a bonus sum of money to keep for themselves and how much to anonymously give to another participant, who was a stranger to them. We found that those who had reflected on experiential purchases were more generous in their giving than those who had thought about material purchases. Experiential purchases seem to orient people outward, making them more kind and helpful; material purchases seem to draw them inward, making them less generous to others.

Live for the Experiences

You might wonder why experiences tend to inspire more gratitude than material possessions. Two reasons are paramount. First, experiences constitute a bigger part of anyone's identity. No matter how much any of us might appreciate our material possessions, they remain separate from us. Experiences, in contrast, are not detached from us: we are, in part, the sum total of our experiences. What we build up in ourselves endures; it doesn't diminish over time. Second, experiences connect us to other people more than our possessions do. We're more likely to join with other people in partaking of experiences, share stories about them, and feel a bond with people who've made the same purchase. These social connections resist adaptation and make the pleasure we get from our experiences endure.

So, the lesson should be clear. If you want to cultivate a more grateful disposition, buy more in the way of experiences and purchase fewer possessions. This does not mean that you need to swear off all material goods and live the life of an ascetic. By all means, continue to enjoy your material possessions. Just shift your expenditures a bit more in the experiential direction and a bit less in the material direction, and you're likely to find yourself enjoying the many psychological benefits that come with being more grateful.

Several modern trends point to an interest in curbing our materialistic spending, from environmental awareness to new approaches toward urban planning. It is my hope that our research on the greater gratitude and satisfaction that people derive from experiential over material consumption will add another voice to this emerging chorus.

What remains to be done is to conduct research on how these findings can be scaled up. For example, when communities invest in experiential infrastructure (parks, trails, beaches, amphitheaters), does the population as a whole achieve a gain in well-being and gratitude? And as advances in robotics and artificial intelligence lead to the elimination of more and more manufacturing jobs—which provide consumers with material goods—might new experiential jobs arise to fill the gaps?

I am excited about the prospect of finding out—and of contributing to a growing social movement that will lead to a less materialist and more experiential economy.

PART 6

Conversations About the Transformative Potential of Gratitude

The pages that follow look at the bigger picture. Some of these essays explore research about gratitude's potential to reduce materialism, restore social trust, and raise political engagement. The contributors also talk with thinkers like Jack Kornfeld, W. Kamau Bell, and Brother David Steindl-Rast about how gratitude can be used to confront global suffering, build opposition to that suffering, and perhaps carve out a path to a better world.

The portrait that emerges from these essays and interviews is of a society at odds with itself. On the one hand, we crave connection; on the other, many of us are desperately afraid of other people. We don't want to depend on anyone. We can also simply be afraid of strangers and what they want. This is a conflict that rages between groups of people, and yet, at the same time, it is also one that many of us feel raging inside of our heads: *Do I trust that person? Do I believe that voting will make a difference? Is it really so terrible if I put the new TV on my credit card?*

At each of these decision points, an attitude of gratitude can help us make healthier choices—choices whose impact goes well beyond our individual lives. When we hear "thank you," we learn we matter—and we know, if only unconsciously, that it will help other people feel like they matter if they hear thanks, too. That creates a chain of gratitude that research suggests will make everyone happier and healthier.

Our society will continue to face serious problems and threats, like global warming and inequality. But, perhaps, if we feel more connected to each other and grateful for what we have, we'll have more strength and resilience to address them.

CHAPTER 23

Can Gratitude Confront Suffering?

A Conversation with Jack Kornfield

By Jill Suttie

When we're deluged by bad-news stories, it's hard to not feel discouraged or even depressed. But, according to Buddhist psychologist Jack Kornfield, falling into despair is not a response that helps anyone—neither you nor your community nor the world. Instead, he argues, we must aim for compassion, caring, and equanimity.

In this conversation, the acclaimed author of books like *A Path with Heart* and *The Wise Heart* offers up his perspective on suffering and what we can do to maintain our caring heart, using practices honed over thousands of years from ancient wisdom traditions. Many of these practices have been validated by researchers studying the new science of personal and social well-being, suggesting an interesting confluence between ancient traditions and modern science.

Jill Suttie: How do you define happiness?

Jack Kornfield: Happiness has lots of meanings. We're happy if there's safety and security in our life, and we're happy in the deepest way when we feel a sense of belonging and connection with one another, and with the beautiful world around us. We're happy if we have a sense of purpose and meaning; we're happy if we can learn to tend our own heart and mind in a way that brings inner well-being and peace and joy amidst the vicissitudes of life.

Happiness in the deepest sense is not a feeling state or a succession of pleasures but a deep sense of well-being and an appreciation for life itself, with all of its mystery and changes.

JS: How can we find happiness when there is so much suffering in the world?

JK: There is inevitably suffering in every human life, and nothing insulates us from this—no amount of money, success, fame, or accomplishment. But it's possible to cultivate and develop a sense of well-being, joy, deep happiness, and worth, even amidst the difficulties of life. I've been in the poorest refugee camps and seen people move with more dignity, connection to others, and love than in circumstances of tremendous wealth and prosperity.

If you go to work in a refugee camp, it doesn't help the people there if you are depressed or unhappy. When you are working with people in difficulty, they don't want you to come with your fears and confusion.

Yes, compassion is important; but joy is also important—it is what the French philosopher André Gide called "a moral obligation." Our gift to the world comes as much through our being and presence, our smile and touch, our sense of possibility and the mystery of human life, as it does in the specifics of what we do. Wherever we go, we can be a beacon of well-being, love, and care that not only touches but also uplifts those whom we encounter.

The Greater Good Science Center is part of a new movement in Western psychology toward positive states, drawing on capacities built into the ancient wisdom traditions of the world. Buddhist psychology is the opposite of the medical model of Western psychology, which focuses on diagnosing and healing pathology. Buddhist psychology is focused on human well-being and offers practical ways to build joy, caring, compassion, a peaceful heart, a liberated spirit, and an inner sense of freedom among the vicissitudes of life.

Modern neuroscience confirms that we can learn to steady our attention, quiet our minds, and open our hearts in a systematic way. Simple practices of mindfulness, gratitude, forgiveness, joy, and compassion positively affect our health and well-being and beneficially affect all those we touch. These states are our birthright; they are possible for us as human beings.

JS: But there must be challenges to living more joyfully. How can we overcome them?

JK: Part of what may get in the way is that we feel it's wrong to have an inner happiness. When there's ongoing injustice in the world—grain elevators full of food while children are starving; conflicts and fears of terrorism, while we continue to sell billions of dollars of weapons and spread them around the globe—we all know something's wrong with this picture.

The world doesn't need more food—we have plenty to share—and it doesn't need more weapons. It needs more care and connection; it needs more love. We know this as surely as we know our own name. And yet, because we can't change all of this at once, we feel overwhelmed, guilty, or ashamed, or that it's not right for us to have a measure of happiness.

In a remarkable poem by poet Jack Gilbert called "A Brief for the Defense," he says: "We must have the stubbornness to accept our gladness in the ruthless furnace of this world. To make injustice the only measure of our attention is to praise the devil."

It doesn't mean that we don't do all we can to make a difference—to stretch our arms and mend the places we can with our own given capacities, to plant good seeds, to stand up for justice, to heal what is broken. This is part of what gives us meaning and well-being. But to do so with a joyful heart is a very different thing than to act out of anger, guilt, fear, or despair.

JS: Is there a role for gratitude in finding happiness during hard times?

JK: Gratitude and appreciation are a deep dimension of happiness. Our media and our news tend to focus on the problems—a bombing, an earthquake, a murder, or a conflict—but these are actually anomalies. Each time there is a bad piece of news that gets publicized, there are a hundred million acts of goodness that happen in that same hour—people putting a plate of cooked spaghetti in front of their child, people stopping at a red light so you can safely pass on the green, people planting gardens and designing new homes, millions of acts of goodness. Then there's the beauty of life itself, where even after a rainstorm, we see the lavender reflections of the sunset in the puddles in the street.

If we pay attention with a tender heart, we can see the eyes of passersby—sometimes weary, sometimes hurried—with all of their humanity on display. There are always birds in the sky and the dazzling display of clouds, weather, blueness, and stars that meet our uplifted eyes. How can we not see the mystery of incarnation and appreciate life?

If you step into the street, and a car comes rushing by, you jump onto the curb to save your life—you care about your life. Every cell of your body carries this appreciation. Gratitude is loving attention that brings into the heart the sense that we belong here in this life. And, with each step, each smile, each gesture, we can add our gift and add our part in small and large ways.

JS: People sometimes have trouble accessing gratitude, though, right?

JK: The mind has a million channels. We can tune in to the channels of depression and fear, or we can tune in to the channels of connection and love. Our brain is wired this way. We have a primitive brain that is easily activated into a fight, flight, or freeze response. Much of the modern news cycle works to capture our attention by trying to scare us. This is the aim of modern politics, too. We can all feel the growing level of anxiety in our culture and globally.

But there are other channels. In that same moment, we can see the fiction and the manipulation that often accompany politics and the media's attempt to scare us and capture our attention through our fears. We can also look around and see that there is enormous beauty in the world and zillions of acts of kindness at the very same time. Depending on what seeds we water and where we direct our attention, we can live in fear and confusion or we can activate many other powerful dimensions of our own heart and mind—of caring, confidence, equanimity, and well-being. These are innate in us and, with care, can be enhanced and awakened.

In my decades of working as a Buddhist teacher and psychologist, I've seen how even a little training in compassion, gratitude, generosity, mindfulness, and loving awareness can change a difficult situation in moments. Whatever seeds we water will grow in our minds and hearts.

JS: Do you think that individuals practicing gratitude impact those around them? If so, how?

JK: How could it not? It's a joy to spread well-being, but it's also a moral force. When the Zen master Thich Nhat Hanh explained this, he said that when the crowded refugee boats met with storms and pirates, if everyone panicked, all would be lost. But if even one person in the boat remained centered and calm, it was enough to show the way for everyone to survive. We become that person on the boat of the world when we center ourselves with a peaceful heart, with a spirit of care and well-being. This affects all those around us.

Though gratitude is a beautiful quality, I don't know if it's the right word. I think caring is what we're looking for—caring for yourself, for this life, the human community, the earth, for one another. Caring has love, awareness, gratitude, and appreciation all in it.

You ask, can changing your inner life make a difference in the troubles of the world? Nothing else can! No amount of technology, computers, internet, artificial intelligence, biotech, nanotechnology, or space technology is going to stop continuing racism, warfare, environmental destruction, and tribalism. These all have their source in the human heart.

The outer developments that are so remarkable in our human world now need to be matched by the inner developments of humanity. These inner developments can awaken compassion for ourselves and others. They grow from loving attention and awareness—they develop a deep sense of interconnection, of care and social and emotional wisdom. This is the great task of modern times. To bring the inner level of human consciousness up to the level of our outer development. Nothing else will really make a difference.

Can Gratitude Make Society More Trusting?

By Elizabeth Hopper

Research suggests that over the past few decades Americans have become less trusting of each other, of institutions like corporations and the press, of government, and more. That's a problem. Trust has numerous benefits for individuals and societies, such as healthier relationships, lower crime, and even a better economy. So how can we reverse this trend?

A study suggests that increasing feelings of gratitude is one potential way. In the study, published in the journal *Personality and Individual Differences*, researchers found that people who had consciously counted their blessings for just a week were more likely to trust others. The researchers asked half of the participants to complete a gratitude journal. Every three days, they listed up to five things for which they felt grateful; the other half of the participants simply wrote about what they had done over the past several days. Everyone completed a total of three journal entries over the course of approximately one week.

Several days after completing their journals, the study participants played a short online "trust game" in the research lab. They were told that they would be exchanging money with another participant playing the game (although, in actuality, the game was played with a computer and there was no other participant). They were given a small amount of money and could choose to give some of this money to the other (fictional) player. They were also told that any money they gave away would be tripled (for example, if they gave away $1, the other player would receive $3) and the other player could choose whether to send any of this windfall back.

Participants who were more trusting of others would presumably give more money to the other person: they would expect to get their money back and that both participants would profit. However, less trusting participants would presumably avoid any risk by keeping the original money for themselves.

The researchers found that participants who had completed the gratitude journaling were more trusting than participants who had simply written about their days. The latter group sent about half of their money (on average) to their partner in the game, while the gratitude group sent almost 70 percent of their money. Participants in the gratitude group also reported feeling more grateful to their partner for sending money back to them. "Raising our ability to appreciate how other people are beneficial in our lives has a downstream consequence of changing the way we relate to strangers," says Todd Kashdan, professor of psychology at George Mason University and a coauthor of the study.

In addition to measuring how much money participants gave to their partner, the researchers measured participants' blood pressure and breathing rate during the interaction to see if there were any physical effects. They found that participants who had written about gratitude had higher systolic blood pressure both while they were deciding how much money to send and when they were waiting to learn how much money their partner had returned to them. Participants in the gratitude group also had faster breathing while waiting for the money to be returned to them and immediately after the money was returned.

You might think that higher blood pressure and faster breathing are signs of stress. But, according to the researchers, they could instead indicate that participants in the gratitude group felt more engaged in the task, or perhaps more enthusiastic about the task, because they expected their generosity to be repaid.

Why did the gratitude group feel more trusting of others? The researchers hypothesized that this higher level of trust could be due to positive emotions: participants who had completed the gratitude journal would be expected to feel more positive emotion, and their positive emotions would cause them to be more trusting. The researchers indeed found support for this. Participants who had completed the gratitude journal reported higher levels of positive emotions during the trust game, and these feelings accounted for their decision to trust their partner with more money.

"It seems unfathomable that such small interventions could have such broad effects," says Kashdan. But, as so many essays in this book describe, his is one of many studies that bear out the wide-ranging benefits of gratitude.

Can Gratitude Beat Materialism?

By Dacher Keltner and Jason Marsh

You know that social scientists are concerned about something when they create a scale to measure it. In the early 1990s, researchers Marsha Richins and Scott Dawson developed such a scale to measure materialism rigorously for the first time. According to this scale, people are materialistic to the extent that they place acquiring possessions at the center of their lives, judge success by the number and quality of their possessions, and see these possessions as vital to happiness (for instance, they agree with statements like "My life would be better if I owned certain things I don't have").

For more than two decades, studies have consistently found that people who score high on Richins and Dawson's scale score lower on just about every major scale that scientists use to measure happiness. For instance, a 1992 study by Richins and Dawson themselves, published in the *Journal of Consumer Research*, found that more materialistic people feel less satisfied both with their lives as a whole and with the amount of fun and enjoyment they get out of day-to-day life. More recently, a study by Todd Kashdan and William Breen, published in the *Journal of Social and Clinical Psychology*, found that materialistic people experience more negative emotion (such as fear and sadness), less positive emotion, and less meaning in their lives.

In trying to understand why materialism undermines our pursuit of happiness, scientists have zeroed in on the fact that more materialistic people report particularly low levels of gratitude. In 2014, Jo-Ann Tsang of Baylor University and her colleagues surveyed 246 undergraduate students to measure their levels of materialism, life satisfaction, and gratitude. Their results, published in the journal *Personality and Individual Differences*, show that as materialism increased, feelings of gratitude and life satisfaction decreased. Further analysis revealed that more materialistic participants felt less satisfied with their lives mainly because they were experiencing less gratitude.

Why are gratitude and materialism opposing forces in the mind? As we know from the work of Robert Emmons—mentioned many times in this book—gratitude involves acknowledging the good things in our lives, from the beauty of autumn leaves to the generosity of friends to the taste of a good meal, and recognizing the other people or forces that made them possible. Gratitude helps us savor the good in our lives rather than take it for granted while yearning for what's next. One of the traps of materialism, by contrast, is that it locates sources of happiness in shiny new things. Indeed, research suggests that materialistic people have unrealistically high expectations for the amount of happiness material goods will bring them. When those expectations inevitably go unmet, they invest their hopes for happiness in the next thing, and the thing after that, on and on in a fruitless pursuit.

Our evolved capacity for gratitude by no means guarantees that we'll reliably practice gratitude—sometimes culture gets in the way. Jo-Ann Tsang's work suggests this is exactly what happens when people develop more materialistic values: their feelings of gratitude get edged out.

The good news, though, is that the relationship between materialism and gratitude can run in the opposite direction. A 2009 study led by Dr. Nathaniel Lambert found that inducing gratitude in people caused them to focus less on acquiring material possessions. Lambert and his colleagues were able to increase gratitude in their participants by instructing them to focus on appreciating the good things they had been given in life, then write about what came to mind.

As Tom Gilovich reports in "How to Help Other People Become More Grateful" in part 5, people report feeling more grateful for experiential purchases than for material purchases. This suggests that spending money isn't necessarily antithetical to gratitude and happiness. What matters is how you spend it—and that you take a moment to give thanks for what you have.

CHAPTER 24

Can Gratitude Bring Americans Back Together?

A Conversation with W. Kamau Bell

By Jeremy Adam Smith

W. Kamau Bell has carved out an unusual niche for himself in today's polarized social and political landscape. He's a comedian with real moral seriousness, a black man who reveals the lives of people who hate him, and a social commentator who tries to tear down barriers rather than build them up. Through his autobiographical stand-up specials like *Private School Negro* and his best-selling book, *The Awkward Thoughts of W. Kamau Bell*, he's explored how social forces have shaped his personality and life. Through his CNN series, *United Shades of America*, he's encouraged extremely diverse groups of Americans to speak for themselves and explain their own lives, decisions, and values.

Unlike many of his peers in comedy, Bell isn't bombastic, and he's relatively unsarcastic. Instead, he's created a persona that is self-deprecating, modest, patient, compassionate, and curious—all qualities he brought to bear in this conversation about the place of gratitude in a divided America.

Jeremy Adam Smith: What are you grateful for these days?

W. Kamau Bell: I've got three kids. They're healthy. I've got a seven-year-old, an almost four-year-old, a twelve-week-old. I'm grateful that my oldest likes school. I think it's a gift to not look at school as a burden but as a fun place to go to. Grateful that my wife figured out how to have the twelve-week-old and have a job at the University of San Francisco teaching, and figured out how to hold it down while my work takes me on the road constantly. And I'm grateful that we just moved my mom from Indiana to up here in Oakland, so she can see her grand-kids whenever she wants to.

Last year, when I won an Emmy, I was like, "What? Excuse me?" I didn't expect to win an Emmy, because that was not on my list of things to do. When my wife and I were on the plane coming home, I said, "We should just email all our friends and see if they just want to come over and take pictures with the Emmy," because it's just this thing, this physicalized example of your success. My kids call it a trophy. I feel super grateful about it. I know that it means something, if it means people in my industry think I'm doing good work. It also means that if my show gets canceled, somebody will give me something else to do because I won an Emmy! I'm grateful that it'll help me provide for my family.

But I also think it's silly. I wanted my friends to be a part of this, so we invited them to a playground across the street from our house. They were like, "Can I touch it?" And I'd say, "Yeah, you can touch it, take a picture with it." All these people took pictures with the Emmy. That helped me feel grateful, because I wasn't thinking, *It's my Emmy and nobody else won this Emmy but me.* Instead, it's like this: *These are the people in my life who have been around to help support me as I made this long march toward this career.*

JAS: What do you find people thank *you* for?

WKB: I feel like the thank-yous I get the most often are from people who are fans of either *United Shades* or my stand-up, or any entertainment media stuff I've done. They'll say, "Thank you for exposing me to stuff that I had no idea of," or "Thank you for highlighting a community I'm a part of that never gets highlighted..." Those are the two big ones. I hear them in airports, because I get stuck in airports a lot. That's my number one recognize location.

JAS: Yeah, I'd probably thank you in an airport, too.

WKB: Sometimes they say, "Thank you for your bravery," which I think is overplayed. People think I'm braver than I am. Like, "You really went to that place to do that thing." But yeah, I get thanked for that.

JAS: Do your wife and your kids and your mother just grunt at you and never thank you for anything?

WKB: No, they say thank-you all the time. It's a big priority in our parenting. When I put the kids to bed, some nights I'll go, "Okay, tell me three things you feel gratitude about today." We taught the girls gratitude at an early age and what it means. Just put that idea in their head that you have to be grateful. I also have a thing I say to my daughters: "You can't say thank-you enough to somebody." They know how to say thank-you, but sometimes they forget or they're too quiet about it. I'll remind them: "Say thank-you." They're like, "I did." And I'll be like, "Say it again." Nobody gets annoyed about somebody saying thank-you too often.

JAS: That's pretty interesting that you try to cultivate some gratitude at home with your kids.

WKB: Yeah. My oldest daughter, who's seven, was born right before I got my first big show-biz opportunity—my first television show. She has grown up with me being on TV and being around celebrities. We travel a lot and she sees people stop me in the street. I feel a big pressure to make sure she doesn't think this is normal. My career gives us access to a lot of people and places and things, and I just think that it would be really easy, if my career continues on this trajectory, to raise privileged assholes. So, I'm just trying to actively not raise assholes. My kids aren't assholes, though. But I feel a big pressure to make sure our life doesn't go to their heads. Gratitude helps us all keep our feet on the ground.

JAS: On *United Shades of America*, you've hung out with spring breakers and retirees in Florida, Klansmen, prisoners, Indigenous Alaskans, Latinos in Los Angeles, hippies and survivalists living off the grid. Do the people you've interviewed express gratitude? What for?

WKB: As we're shooting it? Yeah. We'll hear from people, especially when the show first started, people didn't really know what they were getting into. Like, "Oh, it's a black man shooting a documentary series, this comedian, but I don't know who he is. All right, let's give it a shot." Then, usually after the interview—when they realize I'm usually making them laugh and I'm not making fun of them—they get to have fun with it. Then, they get to make me laugh, and then a lot of times people are like, "Oh, that was fun. Thank you." It's important for me and the crew to make the experience fun and easy for them, because that will make them better on camera, and then also the more relaxed we are, the better the whole thing goes.

We did an episode about the Sikh community, and they were really grateful, as a group. They said, "Thank you for doing this. We've never been featured that way." I met a couple Sikhs after a show one night, and one guy gave me the iron bracelet they wear around their wrist, which is something they're supposed to have on all the time. He took his off and gave it to me and said, "You understand how important this is." That blew me away. I get blown away all the time by how important the show is to people, and how important it is for them to show me how important it is to them.

JAS: I'm curious if you recall whether the Klansmen or [white supremacist leader] Richard Spencer thanked you when you shot their episodes.

WKB: Yes. I would say Richard Spencer thanked me in the way that you would thank somebody after a business meeting: "Thank you, this was good." He enjoyed his time in the interview. I just wasn't as argumentative with him as other people would be. I probably thanked him and the Klan for their time. Some of that is me performing, like, "Oh, thanks guys, see you later," which is what you do when you're trying to get out alive. But with Spencer and the Klan, we didn't leave in a tense, rough situation. It felt friendly. I definitely felt like…it's weird. I feel like with some of these Klan members, I could come back tomorrow and be like, "Hey guys, I just came to hang out." And they'd be like, "Oh, good to see you again." Of course, I didn't want to test that theory.

JAS: How did it make you feel when Spencer thanked you? Or did you feel anything?

WKB: It felt like this is what you're supposed to do. I pushed back on things, but it didn't get tense in any way. Spencer likes to be the friendly, charismatic white supremacist. So, it's part of his thing to say, "Well, thank you for talking to me." *See, I don't hate you. I'm not mad at you because you're black*—or whatever. But I didn't think, *Man, he was so much nicer than I expected.* It just felt like, *Yeah, this is what the guy's supposed to do. He's the kinder, gentler white supremacist.* At least that's how he's marketing himself. Later, he tweeted at me, and I felt like, *I don't need to go tweeting back and forth with Richard Spencer like we're friends.*

JAS: Do you think of Donald Trump as a grateful person?

WKB: No. That's probably one of his biggest problems, that he's filled with not-gratitude. I think that you can't get to be the guy he is and the way he performs himself in the world without having a lack of gratitude.

JAS: Well, I did some investigative reporting in preparation for this interview. I went to Donald Trump's Twitter feed, and I counted his expressions of gratitude since July 1 of this year. I found sixty expressions of gratitude. Then I went to the Twitter feed of another reality-TV star, W. Kamau Bell…

WKB: Uh-oh.

JAS: …and I found just twenty-seven expressions of gratitude, many of which were actually sarcastic, in the same time period—less than half of the president's expressions.

WKB: It's funny, I don't think of Twitter as being where I go to express my gratitude.

JAS: Right. I think of Twitter as being the most antisocial place in the world.

WKB: Yes. And professions of gratitude on social media are often performative.

JAS: Absolutely.

WKB: You're doing it so other people see it. You're so, *Hey, everybody…* And also, I wonder how many times Donald Trump was thanking somebody for saying something nice about him, or…

JAS: Oh yeah, almost always.

WKB: …being with him, or defending him. You know what I mean?

JAS: Yeah. Your perception is correct, at least for the period I looked at.

WKB: I talk to my daughters about this: "You can't say thank-you for quid pro quo. You can't be thankful with conditions."

JAS: On Twitter, Trump often scolds people for being ungrateful, and almost always they are people of color—often black athletes or black people associated with athletics. I think the most striking example is when the president of the United States called LaVar Ball "an ungrateful fool." What do you make of that?

WKB: I'd like to ask Trump, "Okay, how do you define gratefulness?" Because I think how he defines it is not the way that most people I know define gratefulness. When he's saying LaVar Ball's an ungrateful fool, he's basically saying, "Somebody created your success for you, and you're just there to witness your own success." Not about you working hard or you being savvy or you being intelligent. It's about the fact that you lucked into the fact that you're LaVar Ball. When it's like, you don't luck into that, I'm sure, and whoever he needs to be grateful to has nothing to do with Donald Trump.

JAS: Trump seems to weaponize gratitude. It's something he uses to elevate his friends and attack his enemies.

WKB: If any black person of any note says something good about him, then he's like, "Thank you."

JAS: Yeah, he retweets it.

WKB: He's saying, "This one is doing it the right way. The rest of you are wrong."

JAS: In *United Shades of America*, you're going out to all parts of the country and talking with many different kinds of people. Do you feel that our society is really as polarized as it seems to be if you're looking at Twitter or Facebook?

WKB: No, because I think a lot of times—and again, we're talking about the performative nature of social media—people will say things on social media that they won't say to each other when they're standing in the same room. They might say it if they're in a crowd and the other person is in the crowd—or you're in a crowd and the other person is by themselves—then it can be performative. But a lot of times, if you sit down with these people and go, "Okay, let's do this," animosity starts to melt away. I think that a lot of social media is like team sports, where you just rah-rah your team and you shit on the other team. Nuance does not enter into that context, which is why I think a lot of people have started to leave Facebook, because it's like, "This is just too much. It's all dragging me down."

JAS: You seem to believe that social media is a force for polarization.

WKB: I think the algorithm is pushing us toward polarization. I think that's what it is. Sometimes we think of social media as the power company or the cable company, or some sort of benign force: "I would like cable in my house," or "I would like electricity." But these things are owned by people. Do you know what I mean? You think of the water company as there for the public good, and every house gets water, no matter what is happening, and we think of social media as being somehow part of the public good—and it's not. Social media are corporations owned by people with very particular agendas. I think social media could be changed so that it was leaning more toward being a force for good. But right now, we need people who want to use it as a force to do good, to work to push it in that direction, because it's not going there on its own.

JAS: Based on this experience with *United Shades*, what do you think is going to bring us back together?

WKB: I believe that if we look at where America started at versus where America is now, we can see that the country always moves in a more open and equitable direction. Sometimes, it moves slowly, and sometimes it takes steps back—and right now we're in a step-back era. I don't think we'll continue to go back, but it takes the work of many, many people to get going again in the right direction. We didn't just get this Civil Rights Bill of 1968 because it was gonna happen. The Civil Rights Bill happened because Martin Luther King was like, "Go out in the streets, black people," and other people joined them.

The work has to be done. I come from a line of people who did the work. Even though I'm just a simple comedian, it still feels like if I'm not involved in making the world better somehow, then I'm wasting my time and slowing progress down. I try to do the work onstage and off-stage and with my kids. It's this multilayered attack. In my work, I try to pull in the direction I think is a better direction, and I believe I should take some of my resources to actually help people—now that I have some money and some privilege—to actually help elevate people. At home, it's like, "Kids, let's talk about gratitude before you go to sleep."

JAS: Moving forward can involve conflict. When you feel yourself to be in conflict with people, it's hard to be grateful, if only because the stress makes you a lot more self-focused. And we at *Greater Good* hear from people who argue that gratitude breeds complacency: the more grateful you are for what you have, the less likely you are to act to change it. Is that something you'd agree with?

WKB: No, I don't think gratitude breeds complacency. I feel like it's quite the opposite. It's a lack of gratitude that breeds complacency. To me, if you're truly grateful for what you have, that means you know that, on some level, you don't really deserve it—and therefore, if you don't deserve it, you should probably try to create a lot more gratitude in the world so that everybody can be grateful. You know what I mean? I think that true gratitude, as I understand it, is to feel lucky and to feel like, *Wow, this is so cool this happened.*

Gratitude Encourages Voting

By Jill Suttie

Political psychology researchers have been studying what encourages voting behavior, hoping to create interventions that might increase voting in the general public. "Because voting is a prosocial behavior, the kinds of things that should stimulate other types of prosocial behavior should have similar impacts on voting," says Costas Panagopoulos of Northeastern University. In one study, Panagopoulos sent postcards to a subset of random voters before a special election in New York and before a gubernatorial election in New Jersey. The postcards contained either a message encouraging people to vote or a message thanking them for having voted in a recent election. Then he compared voting percentages for those two groups to a control group that received no postcards.

His findings showed that voters receiving the gratitude postcard voted significantly more—2 to 3 percentage points more—than those not receiving postcards. Those receiving simple reminders were somewhere in the middle, voting only slightly more often than the control group. This held true whether or not the recipients tended to vote regularly or only sparingly, including voters from groups who tend to vote less frequently, in general—like Latinos and single women.

Why would this be? "Making people feel good by reinforcing the notion that society is grateful for their participation in the political process reminds people that they have a role to play and reinforces their willingness to be responsive," says Panagopoulos. Though the increase might seem inconsequential, says Panagopoulos, elections are won and lost within that margin. Even going door-to-door to get out the vote—a typical, resource-intensive strategy for increasing voter turnout—rarely increases voting by more than 8 to 10 percentage points, making a gratitude postcard a good investment.

"The fact that you can achieve almost a third of that with a single postcard mailing is pretty huge," he says. It's roughly five times the effect of a generic postcard mailer reminding someone to vote. So the expression of gratitude must be a pretty powerful way to raise turnout." Still, even with these results, Panagopoulos wanted to make sure that receiving thanks was the active ingredient; after all, the postcards implied that someone was paying attention to people's voting behavior, and public scrutiny could have been a factor.

So, in another experiment, he sent postcards thanking people for political participation, in general—without reference to past voting—while others received either the thanks for voting or the reminder postcards used in the other experiments. In the Georgia primary election that followed, Panagopoulos found that people who received the generic thank-you postcard were as likely to vote or more so than people being specifically thanked for voting and were much more likely to vote than those who got the simple reminders. To Panagopoulos, this confirms the idea that gratitude was key.

"The fact that the generic gratitude message was as effective, if not more effective, than the gratitude message with social pressure elements in it, suggests that what was really doing the work was the expression of gratitude and not any perceptions of surveillance or social pressure," he says.

CHAPTER 25

Is Gratitude the Path to a Better World?

A Conversation with Brother David Steindl-Rast

By Jill Suttie

Long before gratitude became a hot topic of scientific research, the Benedictine monk Brother David Steindl-Rast was writing about gratefulness as the heart of prayer and a path to liberation, helping to promote the practice of gratitude as a way of healing oneself and society. Perhaps best known for helping create interfaith dialogues to increase understanding between religious traditions, he received the Martin Buber Award in 1975 for his work in this area.

Today, he's helping create a worldwide movement called "A Network for Grateful Living" through an interactive online forum that reaches several thousand participants daily from more than 240 countries. He's also the author of numerous books, book chapters, and articles, including 99 *Blessings: An Invitation to Life,* a collection of prayers meant to appeal to a general readership. Few bring deeper knowledge to the topic than Brother David, who, like His Holiness the Dalai Lama, has engaged in regular dialogue with scientists.

Jill Suttie: You began promoting the practice of gratitude for religious reasons long before it became a topic of interest in Western science. What do you make of the sudden scientific interest in studying gratitude?

Brother David Steindl-Rast: Actually, the scientific interest did not arise quite as suddenly as it may seem. As long ago as the mid-twentieth century, alert psychologists like Abraham Maslow became aware of the importance of gratitude—which he writes about in *Religions, Values, and Peak-Experiences*—but mainstream science was stuck in taking physics for its model of inquiry and showed no interest in exploring values. In the twenty-first century, consciousness research and cognitive neuroscience are leading toward new frontiers, encountering new questions, and are beginning to push the envelope of what used to be considered classical scientific inquiry. The change of consciousness that is sweeping the world at large has its effect also on the minds of scientists.

Modern science has the same power over people's minds that religion had in the Middle Ages. But public interest has a more powerful influence on the direction of science than many people realize. For influencing science, an important point of leverage is the funding of research. For example, the Templeton Foundation's funding of Robert Emmons's pioneering studies of grateful behavior has contributed much to making the topic of gratitude acceptable in scientific circles. Scientific findings, in turn, make gratitude respectable in the eyes of the media and so to an ever-growing segment of society. This creates a feedback loop, which accounts for the current "gratitude boom."

JS: Science has shown that practicing gratitude increases happiness and health in an individual. How does practicing gratitude benefit society at large?

BDSR: Well, the first and most obvious answer is, anything that produces happier, healthier individuals thereby creates a society in which more people are healthy and happy. This alone is a great improvement. But we can go a step further and show that grateful individuals live in a way that leads to the kind of society human beings long for. In many parts of the world, society is sick. Keywords of the diagnosis are *exploitation, oppression,* and *violence*. Grateful living is a remedy against all three of these symptoms.

Exploitation springs from greed and a sense of scarcity. Grateful living makes us aware that there is enough for all. Thus, it leads to a sense of sufficiency and a joyful willingness to share with others.

Oppression is necessary if we want to exploit others. It results in competition and in the power pyramid: the more power you have, the more efficiently you can exploit those below you and protect yourself against those above you. But grateful people live with a sense of sufficiency; they need not exploit others. Thus, oppression becomes unnecessary; it is replaced by mutual support and by equal respect for all.

Violence springs from the root of fear—fear that there may not be enough for all, fear of others as potential competitors, fear of foreigners and strangers. But the grateful person is fearless. Thereby, she cuts off the very root of violence. Out of a sense of enough, she is willing to share and thereby tends to eliminate the unjust distribution of wealth that creates the climate for violence. Fearlessly, she welcomes the new and strange, finds herself enriched by differences, and celebrates variety.

Thus, grateful living takes away the main reasons for exploitation, oppression, and violence; through sharing, universal respect, and non-violence, it provides the basis for a healthy society and a world with a chance to survive.

JS: Some people think the science of gratitude is a waste of time—in other words, it's obvious that gratitude is good for you. Do you think science contributes something important to the global gratitude movement? If so, what are its contributions?

BDSR: We all know that eating is not only good for us but also necessary for survival. And yet, the scientific study of nutrition can bring us great benefits. Similarly, although everyone knows that it feels good to be grateful, the scientific study of gratitude can broaden our knowledge, refine our distinctions, and deepen our understanding.

Just as academic interest gave nutrition a new respectability, it can do the same for gratitude. This is important and can certainly be of help to the global gratitude movement. However, what gives a movement its impetus is not information but enthusiasm and commitment. The spark that ignited the global gratitude movement is the enthusiasm of men and women who discovered that grateful living makes life meaningful and full of joy.

JS: Some people may experience difficulty practicing gratitude, maybe because they're depressed or they've experienced a severe trauma. What advice would you give to someone in that state of mind?

BDSR: Gratitude is the spontaneous response of a healthy body and mind to life. We should not expect it from a person who suffers in mind or body. With training, however, one can learn to focus on *opportunity* as the gift within every given moment. This attitude toward life always improves the situation. Even in times of sickness, someone who habitually practices grateful living will look for the opportunity that a given moment offers and use it creatively.

JS: Do you ever have days where it's hard for you to practice gratitude? If so, what gets in your way?

BDSR: Illness and depression make it more difficult to be alert to gratitude, for lack of energy. But even on healthy days, I need to put myself back, again and again, onto the track of grateful living. What gets in the way is familiarity. The proverb is right: "Familiarity breeds contempt." Grateful eyes look at whatever it be as if they had never seen it before and caress it as if they would never see it again. This is a most realistic attitude, for every moment is indeed unique. But of this, I need to remind myself again and again. This reminding myself is the dynamic element in mindfulness.

Grateful living is the awareness that we stand on holy ground—always—in touch with Mystery. Jewish sages interpret the words of Genesis 3:5 in a way that is of great relevance to grateful living: "Take off your shoes; the ground on which you stand is holy ground." The soles of your shoes are leather—dead animal skin. Take off the deadness of being used to it, and your live souls will feel that you are standing on holy ground, wherever you are.

JS: Where do you see the gratitude movement heading from here?

BDSR: As someone aptly quipped, "It is difficult to make predictions—especially about the future." It is, however, pretty evident that greed, oppression, and violence have led us to a point of self-destruction. Our survival depends on a radical change; if the gratitude movement grows strong and deep enough, it may bring about this necessary change. Grateful living brings in place of greed, sharing; in place of oppression, respect; in place of violence, peace. Who does not long for a world of sharing, mutual respect, and peace?

Contributors

Maryam Abdullah, PhD, is the parenting program director of the Greater Good Science Center (GGSC). She is a developmental psychologist with expertise in parent-child relationships and children's development of prosocial behaviors. Prior to joining GGSC, she was an assistant project scientist at the University of California, Irvine, Child Development School in the Department of Pediatrics, a school-based behavioral health program, where she provided parenting and child interventions, oversaw clinical outcomes and program evaluation, and mentored undergraduate students with research projects. Her research experiences include exploration of parent-child relationships, early development of children with autism spectrum disorder, and traditional behavioral and canine-assisted interventions for attention deficit hyperactivity disorder. She was the recipient of the UCI Health ARIISE Award for Respect.

Jess Alberts, PhD, is President's Professor in the Hugh Downs School of Human Communication at Arizona State University. Her research interests include conflict, relationship communication, and the division of labor.

Sara Algoe, PhD, is an assistant professor in the department of psychology and neuroscience at the University of North Carolina at Chapel Hill. There, she is the director of the Emotions and Social Interactions in Relationships Laboratory. Her expertise spans emotions, relationships, and health psychology. Some of her most cited work is related to her development of the find-remind-and-bind theory of gratitude, which—at its core—posits that the emotional response of gratitude helps solve a central problem of human survival: identifying high-quality relationship partners and keeping them interested in the relationship.

Summer Allen, PhD, was a research and writing fellow with the Greater Good Science Center. A graduate of Carleton College and Brown University, Summer now writes for a variety of publications, including weekly blog posts for the American Association for the Advancement of Science.

Christina Armenta, PhD, is a researcher with the Positive Activities and Well-Being Lab at the University of California, Riverside. Her research focuses on whether positive activities, such as expressing gratitude, can motivate self-improvement efforts. Most of her work has explored this phenomenon in applied settings such as workplaces and high schools around the world.

Giacomo Bono, PhD, is an assistant professor at California State University, Dominguez Hills, who studies positive youth development with an emphasis on prosocial behavior and relationships. He is the coauthor, with Jeffrey Froh, of *Making Grateful Kids: The Science of Building Character.*

Joshua Brown, PhD, is a professor of psychological and brain sciences at Indiana University in Bloomington. His research interests include functional neuroimaging, higher cognitive function, addiction, and computational neural modeling.

Catherine Brozena has been serving the nonprofit, public health, environmental, and education sectors as a communications professional for more than fifteen years. She is the founder and creative director for ColorThisWorld Communications, a mission-driven communications consultancy dedicated to lifting up stories and ideas that convey substance, arouse meaning, and inspire positive social change. Her work has spanned everything from developing communications strategies that activate audiences on broad public health and environmental stewardship campaigns to providing hands-on communications support through blogs, infographics, websites, videos, social media messages, and more.

Christine Carter, PhD, is a senior fellow at the Greater Good Science Center. She is the author of *The New Adolescence: Raising Happy and Successful Teens in an Age of Anxiety and Distraction* (BenBella, 2020), *The Sweet Spot: How to Accomplish More by Doing Less* (Ballantine Books, 2015), and *Raising Happiness: 10 Simple Steps for More Joyful Kids and Happier Parents* (Random House, 2010).

David DeSteno, PhD, is a professor of psychology at Northwestern University and is the author of *Emotional Success* and *The Truth About Trust*, and coauthor of a *Wall Street Journal* spotlight psychology bestseller, *Out of Character.*

Robert Emmons, PhD, is the world's leading scientific expert on gratitude. He is a professor of psychology at the University of California, Davis, and the founding editor in chief of the *Journal of Positive Psychology*. He is the author of *Thanks! How the New Science of Gratitude Can Make You Happier; Gratitude Works! A 21-Day Program for Creating Emotional Prosperity;* and *The Little Book of Gratitude.*

Glenn Fox, PhD, is the head of program design, strategy, and outreach at the Performance Science Institute at University of Southern California. He earned his doctorate from Antonio Damasio at USC's Neuroscience Graduate Program. His current research focuses on the relationships among emotion, health, and performance in day-to-day settings.

Megan M. Fritz is a postdoctoral research fellow at the University of Pittsburgh. Her work focuses on the capacity of positive activities, such as practicing kindness and gratitude, to improve (or undermine) individuals' well-being and physical health.

Jeffrey Froh, PsyD, is an associate professor at Hofstra University, with primary responsibilities in the PsyD in School-Community Psychology program. His son wrote his first thank-you letter at the age of three months.

Tom Gilovich, PhD, is a professor of psychology at Cornell University. His research deals with how people evaluate the evidence of their everyday experience to make judgments, form beliefs, and decide on courses of action, and how they sometimes misevaluate that evidence and make faulty judgments, form dubious beliefs, and embark on counterproductive courses of action.

Amie Gordon, PhD, is an assistant professor in social psychology at the University of Michigan, Ann Arbor. She studies the role of prosocial emotions (such as gratitude) and cognitions (such as perspective taking) in close relationships. She also conducts research on the impact of sleep on relationship quality. She received her PhD from the University of California, Berkeley, and her BA from the University of California, Los Angeles.

Nathan Greene, PsyD, is a psychotherapist, researcher, and writer living in Oakland, California. An alumnus of the University of California, Berkeley, and the Wright Institute, he is currently a postdoctoral resident at Westcoast Children's Clinic, where he serves as a psychotherapist and clinical assessor to children, adolescents, and families who have experienced psychological trauma. He also serves as an adjunct clinical faculty member at the Wright Institute, where he offers clinical supervision. His clinical and research interests include childhood trauma, bereavement, resilience, and gratitude. Findings from his study with adults who lost a parent in childhood were published in *Death Studies*, a scientific journal that explores psychological issues related to death, dying, and bereavement.

Leif Hass, MD, is a family medicine doctor who works as a hospitalist in Oakland, California. He also advises the Greater Good Science Center on health care matters.

Elizabeth Hopper, PhD, writes about the science of a meaningful life for *Greater Good Magazine*. She received her PhD in psychology from the University of California, Santa Barbara.

Arianna Huffington is a prolific author and international media mogul who started the award-winning news platform *The Huffington Post*.

Andrea Hussong, PhD, is director of the Center for Developmental Science and a professor of psychology at the University of North Carolina at Chapel Hill. She studies how interactions between parents and kids can foster gratitude.

Christina Karns, PhD, is an assistant research professor at the University of Oregon working at the intersection of emotion, social neuroscience, multisensory integration, attention, and neuroplasticity. Her project "The Grateful Brain: An fMRI study of Generosity and Social Agency Following a Gratitude Intervention" was a gratitude-research grant winner through the Greater Good Science Center and addresses the relationship between gratitude, social reasoning, decision making, and the brain.

Dacher Keltner, PhD, is the founding director of the Greater Good Science Center and a professor of psychology at the University of California, Berkeley. He is the author of *The Power Paradox: How We Gain and Lose Influence* and *Born to Be Good*, and a coeditor of *The Compassionate Instinct*.

Debra Lieberman, PhD, is an associate professor of psychology at the University of Miami. She earned her PhD at the University of California, Santa Barbara, at the Center for Evolutionary Psychology. The central goal of her research is to understand how evolution has shaped the social mind. She studies a range of topics, including kin detection, cooperation, mate choice, disgust, and morality. Most recently, she has been researching gratitude and its role in the formation of cooperative relationships, as well as the role disgust plays in social policy and law. She is coauthor of the book *Objection: Disgust, Morality, and the Law*, published in 2018 by Oxford University Press.

Sonja Lyubomirsky, PhD, is a professor of psychology at the University of California, Riverside, and the author of the best-selling book *The How of Happiness*. She is a leader in the field of positive psychology. Her research has found that people have a strong capacity to determine their own happiness, and she has identified specific, everyday steps people can take to boost their levels of happiness. A graduate of Harvard and Stanford, she has won the esteemed Templeton Positive Psychology Prize and is currently an associate editor of the *Journal of Positive Psychology*. Her teaching has been recognized with the Faculty of the Year award at UC Riverside.

Jason Marsh is the founding editor in chief of *Greater Good Magazine* and Greater Good Science Center's director of programs. He is also a coeditor of two anthologies of *Greater Good* articles: *The Compassionate Instinct* (W. W. Norton, 2010) and *Are We Born Racist?* (Beacon Press, 2010). His writing has also appeared in the *Wall Street Journal*, the *San Francisco Chronicle*, and *Utne Reader*, among other publications, and he writes regularly for the opinion section of CNN.com.

Emily Nauman is a Greater Good Science Center research assistant. She completed her undergraduate studies at Oberlin College with a double major in psychology and French and has previously worked as a research assistant in Oberlin's psycholinguistics lab and Boston University's eating disorders program.

Kira Newman is the managing editor of Greater Good magazine and a former course assistant for the Science of Happiness online course on edX. Her work has been published in outlets including the *Washington Post, Huffington Post, Social Media Monthly,* and *Mindful* magazine. She has created large communities around the science of happiness, including the online course The Year of Happy and the CaféHappy meetup in Toronto. Previously, she was a technology journalist and editor for Tech.Co.

Eric Pedersen, PhD, is an evolutionary social psychologist who studies social cognition and decision making. Some of his main interests include how the mind regulates punishment and anger, how gratitude and forgiveness function to build and maintain cooperative relationships, and how individual and cultural differences in cooperation arise. Eric obtained his BA in psychology from the University of California, Santa Barbara, and his PhD in psychology from the University of Miami. He is an assistant professor of psychology and neuroscience at the University of Colorado, Boulder.

Jeremy Adam Smith edits *Greater Good Magazine.* He is the author of *The Daddy Shift* and coeditor of three anthologies. His coverage of racial and economic segregation in San Francisco schools has won numerous honors, including the Sigma Delta Chi Award for investigative reporting, and he is a three-time winner of the John Swett Award from the California Teachers Association. His articles and essays have appeared in the *San Francisco Chronicle, Scientific American, San Francisco Public Press, Mindful, Wired,* and many other periodicals, websites, and books. Before joining the Greater Good Science Center, Jeremy was a 2010–11 John S. Knight Journalism fellow at Stanford University.

Alex Springer is a research data analyst at the Greater Good Science Center.

Malini Suchak, PhD, is a comparative psychologist studying social cognition, particularly cooperation and social learning, in a variety of species. Currently, she is most interested in better understanding how our companion animals, cats and dogs, make social decisions while living in a multispecies world. Previously, her work focused on social decision making in chimpanzees and capuchin monkeys. She obtained her BS in biology from Canisius College and her MA and PhD in psychology, with an emphasis on neuroscience and animal behavior, from Emory University. She currently resides in Buffalo, New York, where she is an assistant professor of animal behavior, ecology, and conservation at Canisius College.

Jill Suttie, PsyD, is *Greater Good Magazine*'s book review editor and a frequent contributor to the magazine.

Shawn Taylor is a writer, university lecturer, and trainer for behavioral health workers. He has spent more than twenty years working at the intersection of juvenile justice and adolescent mental health.

Angela Trethewey, PhD, is dean of the College of Communication and Education at California State University, Chico.

Joel Wong, PhD, is an associate professor of counseling psychology at Indiana University in Bloomington. His research interests include positive psychology, men and masculinities, and Asian-American mental health.

Bibliography

Listed in chronological order of reference

Part 1. The Roots and Meaning of Gratitude

Chapter 1. What Gratitude Is and Why It Matters, by Robert Emmons with Jeremy Adam Smith

Adapted and revised from two essays for Greater Good Magazine: *"Why Gratitude Is Good" (November 16, 2010) and "Five Myths About Gratitude" (November 21, 2013), both by Robert Emmons.*

Ehrenreich, B. "The Selfish Side of Gratitude." *The New York Times,* December 31, 2015. https://www.nytimes.com/2016/01/03/opinion/sunday/the-selfish-side-of-gratitude.html.

Emmons, R. *THANKS! How the New Science of Gratitude Can Make You Happier.* Boston: Houghton-Mifflin, 2007.

Emmons, R., and M. E. McCullough, eds. *The Psychology of Gratitude.* New York: Oxford University Press, 2004.

Watkins, P. C., K. Woodward, T. Stone, and R. L. Kolts. "Gratitude and Happiness: Development of a Measure of Gratitude and Relationships with Subjective Well-Being." *Social Behavior and Personality: An International Journal* 31, no. 5 (2003): 431–51.

Froh, J. J., G. Bono, and R. Emmons. "Being Grateful Is Beyond Good Manners: Gratitude and Motivation to Contribute to Society Among Early Adolescents." *Motivation and Emotion* 34, no. 2 (2010): 105–214.

Watkins, P. C., L. Cruz, H. Holben, and R. L. Kolts. "Taking Care of Business? Grateful Processing of Unpleasant Memories." *Journal of Positive Psychology* 3, no. 2 (2008): 87–99.

Chow, R. M., and B. S. Lowery. "Thanks, But No Thanks: The Role of Personal Responsibility in the Experience of Gratitude." *Journal of Experimental Social Psychology* 46, no. 3 (2010): 487–93.

Emmons, R., and M. E. McCullough. "Counting Blessings Versus Burdens: An Experimental Investigation of Gratitude and Subjective Well-Being in Daily Life." *Journal of Personality and Social Psychology* 84, no. 2 (2003): 377–89.

Emmons, R., and T. T. Kneezel. "Giving Thanks: Spiritual and Religious Correlates of Gratitude." *Journal of Psychology and Christianity* 24, no. 2 (2005): 140–48.

Bonus. Levels of Gratitude, by Summer Allen

Excerpted and revised from "The Science of Gratitude" (May, 2018), a white paper prepared for the John Templeton Foundation by the Greater Good Science Center at UC Berkeley.

Rosenberg, E. L. "Levels of Analysis and the Organization of Affect." *Review of General Psychology* 2, no. 3 (1998): 247–70.

McCullough, M. E., J. A. Tsang, and R. A. Emmons. "Gratitude in Intermediate Affective Terrain: Links of Grateful Moods to Individual Differences and Daily Emotional Experience." *Journal of Personality and Social Psychology* 86, no. 2 (2004): 295–309.

Chapter 2. Looking for Gratitude's Roots in Primates, by Malini Suchak

Adapted and revised from an essay for Greater Good Magazine: *"The Evolution of Gratitude," by Malini Suchak (February 1, 2017).*

Darwin, C. *The Descent of Man.* London: Penguin Classics, 2004.

Suchak, M., T. M. Eppley, M. W. Campbell, and F. B. M. de Waal. "Ape Duos and Trios: Spontaneous Cooperation with Free Partner Choice in Chimpanzees." *PeerJ* 2, no. e417 (2014): https://doi.org/10.7717/peerj.417.

Tsang, J. A. "Gratitude and Prosocial Behaviour: An Experimental Test of Gratitude." *Cognition and Emotion* 20, no. 1 (2006): 138–48.

Suchak, M., and F. B. M. de Waal. "Monkeys Benefit from Reciprocity Without the Cognitive Burden." *PNAS* 109, no. 38 (2012): 15191–96.

Trivers, R. L. "The Evolution of Reciprocal Altruism." *The Quarterly Review of Biology* 46, no. 1 (1971): 35–57.

Leimgruber K. L., A. F. Ward, J. Widness, M. I. Norton, K. R. Olson, K. Gray, and L. R. Santos. "Give What You Get: Capuchin Monkeys (*Cebus apella*) and 4-Year-Old Children Pay Forward Positive and Negative Outcomes to Conspecifics." *PLoS ONE* 9, no. 1 (2014): e87035.

Nowak, M. A., and S. Roch. "Upstream Reciprocity and the Evolution of Gratitude." *Proceedings of the Royal Society B: Biological Sciences* 274, no. 1610 (2007): 605–10.

Bonus. Do Genes Affect Your Gratitude? by Summer Allen

Excerpted and revised from "The Science of Gratitude" (May, 2018), a white paper prepared for the John Templeton Foundation by the Greater Good Science Center at UC Berkeley.

Steger, M. F., B. M. Hicks, T. B. Kashdan, R. F Krueger, and T. J. Bouchard. "Genetic and Environmental Influences on the Positive Traits of the

Values in Action Classification, and Biometric Covariance with Normal Personality." *Journal of Research in Personality* 41, no. 3 (2007): 524–39.

Algoe, S. B., and B. M. Way. "Evidence for a Role of the Oxytocin System, Indexed by Genetic Variation in CD38, in the Social Bonding Effects of Expressed Gratitude." *Social Cognitive and Affective Neuroscience* 9, no. 12 (2013): 1855–61.

Liu, J., P. Gong, X. Gao, and X. Zhou. "The Association Between Well-Being and the COMT Gene: Dispositional Gratitude and Forgiveness as Mediators." *Journal of Affective Disorders* 214 (2017): 115–21.

Williams, L. M., J. M. Gatt, S. M. Grieve, C. Dobson-Stone, R. H. Paul, E. Gordon, and P. R. Schofield. "COMT Val(108/158)Met Polymorphism Effects on Emotional Brain Function and Negativity Bias." *Neuroimage* 53, no. 3 (2010): 918–25.

Chapter 3. How Gratitude Develops in Us, by Maryam Abdullah, Giacomo Bono, Jeffrey Froh, Andrea Hussong, and Kira Newman

Adapted and revised from four essays for Greater Good *Magazine: "How to Help Gratitude Grow in Your Kids," by Maryam Abdullah (March 13, 2018); "What Parents Neglect to Teach About Gratitude," by Andrea Hussong (November 21, 2017); "What Don't We Know About Gratitude and Youth?" by Giacomo Bono (February 15, 2017); and "Seven Ways to Foster Gratitude in Kids," by Jeffrey Froh and Giacomo Bono (March 5, 2014).*

Nelson, J. A., L. B. de Lucca Freitas, M. O'Brien, S. D. Calkins, E. M. Leerkes, and S. Marcovitch. "Preschool-Aged Children's Understanding of Gratitude: Relations with Emotion and Mental State Knowledge." *British Journal of Developmental Psychology* 31, no. 1 (2013): 42–56.

Halberstadt, A. G., H. A. Langley, A. M. Hussong, W. A. Rothenberg, J. L. Coffman, I. Mokrova, and P. R. Costanzo. "Parents' Understanding of Gratitude in Children: A Thematic Analysis." *Early Childhood Research Quarterly* 36 (3rd quarter 2016): 439–51.

Rothenberg, W. A., A. M. Hussong, H. A. Langley, G. A. Egerton, A. G. Halberstadt, J. L. Coffman, and P. R. Costanzo. "Grateful Parents Raising Grateful Children: Niche Selection and the Socialization of Child Gratitude." *Applied Developmental Science* 21, no. 2 (2017): 106–20.

Hussong, A. M., H. A. Langley, T. Thomas, J. L. Coffman, A. G. Halberstadt, P. R. Costanzo, and W. A. Rothenberg. "Measuring Gratitude in Children." *Journal of Positive Psychology* 14, no. 5 (2019): 563–75.

Hussong, A. M., H. A. Langley, W. A. Rothenberg, J. L. Coffman, A. G. Halberstadt, P. R. Costanzo, and I. Mokrova. "Raising Grateful Children

One Day at a Time." *Applied Developmental Science* 23, no. 4 (2018): 371–84.

Hussong, A. M., H. A. Langley, J. L. Coffman, A. G. Halberstadt, and P. R. Costanzo. "Parent Socialization of Children's Gratitude." In *Developing Gratitude,* edited by J. Tudge and L. Freitas, 199–219. New York: Cambridge University Press, 2018.

Mendonça, S. E., E. A. Merçon-Vargas, A. Payir, and J. R. H. Tudge. "The Development of Gratitude in Seven Societies: Cross-Cultural Highlights." *Cross-Cultural Research* 52, no. 1 (2018): 135–50.

Froh, J. J., G. Bono, J. Fan, R. A. Emmons, K. Henderson, C. Harris, H. Leggio, and A. M. Wood. "Nice Thinking! An Educational Intervention That Teaches Children to Think Gratefully." *School Psychology Review* 43, no. 2 (2014): 132–52.

Chapter 4. What Can the Brain Reveal About Gratitude? by Glenn Fox

Revised from an essay for Greater Good Magazine: *"What Can the Brain Reveal About Gratitude?" by Glenn Fox (August 4, 2017).*

Fox, G. R., J. Kaplan, H. Damasio, and A. Damasio. "Neural Correlates of Gratitude." *Frontiers in Psychology* 6 (2015): 1491.

Henning, M., G. Fox, J. Kaplan, H. Damasio, and A. Damasio. "A Potential Role for Mu-Opioids in Mediating the Positive Effects of Gratitude." *Frontiers in Psychology* 8, no. 868 (2017): https://doi.org/10.3389/fpsyg.2017.00868.

Kini, P., J. Wong, S. McInnis, N. T. Gabana, and J. W. Brown. "The Effects of Gratitude Expression on Neural Activity." *NeuroImage* 128 (2016): 1–10.

Chapter 5. The Surprising Neural Link Between Giving and Gratitude, by Christina Karns

Revised from an essay for Greater Good Magazine: *"Why a Grateful Brain Is a Giving One," by Christina Karns (December 19, 2017).*

McCullough, M. E., S. D. Kilpatrick, R. A. Emmons, and D. B. Larson. "Is Gratitude a Moral Effect?" *Psychological Bulletin* 127, no. 2 (2001): 249–66.

Hubbard, J., W. T. Harbaugh, S. Srivastava, D. Degras, and U. Mayr. "A General Benevolence Dimension That Links Neural, Psychological, Economic, and Life-Span Data on Altruistic Tendencies." *Journal of Experimental Psychology: General* 145, no. 10 (2016): 1351–58.

Karns, C. M., W. E. Moore III, and U. Mayr. "The Cultivation of Pure Altruism Via Gratitude: A Functional MRI Study of Change with Gratitude Practice." *Frontiers in Human Neuroscience* 11 (2017): 599.

Bonus. How Gratitude Relates to Other Emotions, by Summer Allen

Excerpted and revised from "The Science of Gratitude" (May, 2018), a white paper prepared for the John Templeton Foundation by the Greater Good Science Center at UC Berkeley.

Algoe, S. B., and J. Haidt. "Witnessing Excellence in Action: The 'Other-Praising' Emotions of Elevation, Gratitude, and Admiration." *Journal of Positive Psychology* 4, no. 2 (2009): 105–27.

Algoe, S. B., J. Haidt, and S. L. Gable. "Beyond Reciprocity: Gratitude and Relationships in Everyday Life." *Emotion* 8, no. 3 (2008): 425–29.

Adler, M. G., and N. S. Fagley. "Appreciation: Individual Differences in Finding Value and Meaning as a Unique Predictor of Subjective Well-Being." *Journal of Personality* 73, no. 1 (2005): 79–114.

Wood, A. M., S. Joseph, and J. Maltby. "Gratitude Uniquely Predicts Satisfaction with Life: Incremental Validity Above the Domains and Facets of the Five Factor Model." *Personality and Individual Differences* 45, no. 1 (2008): 49–54.

Part 2. The Impact of Gratitude

Chapter 6. Why Gratitude Is Good for Us, by Joel Wong, Joshua Brown, Christina Armenta, Sonja Lyubomirsky, Summer Allen, Amie Gordon, and Kira Newman

Adapted from four essays for Greater Good Magazine: *"How Gratitude Changes You and Your Brain," by Joel Wong and Joshua Brown (June 6, 2017); "How Gratitude Motivates Us to Become Better People," by Christina Armenta and Sonja Lyubomirsky (May 23, 2017); "Is Gratitude Good for Your Health?" by Summer Allen (March 5, 2018); and "Gratitude Is for Lovers," by Amie Gordon (February 3, 2013).*

Watkins, P. "The Social Benefits of Gratitude." *Greater Good Magazine.* September 2014. https://greatergood.berkeley.edu/video/item/ the_social_benefits_of_gratitude.

Berry Mendes, W. "How Does Gratitude Affect Health and Aging?" *Greater Good Magazine.* September 2014. http://greatergood.berkeley.edu/gg_live/ greater_good_gratitude_summit/speaker/wendy_mendes/ how_does_gratitude_affect_health_and_aging/.

Emmons, R. "The Benefits of Gratitude." *Greater Good Magazine.* November 2010. https://greatergood.berkeley.edu/gg_live/science_meaningful_life_ videos/speaker/robert_emmons/the_benefits_of_gratitude.

Watkins, P. C., K. Woodward, T. Stone, and R. L. Kolts. "Gratitude and Happiness: Development of a Measure of Gratitude and Relationships with Subjective Well-Being." *Social Behavior and Personality: An International Journal* 31, no. 5 (2003): 431–52.

Kerr, S. L., A. O'Donovan, and C. A. Pepping. "Can Gratitude and Kindness Interventions Enhance Well-Being in a Clinical Sample?" *Journal of Happiness Studies* 16, no. 1 (2015): 17–36.

Wood, A. M., J. J. Froh, and A. W. A. Geraghty. "Gratitude and Well-Being: A Review and Theoretical Integration." *Clinical Psychology Review* 30, no. 7 (2010): 890–905.

Wong, Y. J., J. Owen, N. T. Gabana, J. W. Brown, S. McInnis, P. Toth, and L. Gilman. "Does Gratitude Writing Improve the Mental Health of Psychotherapy Clients? Evidence from a Randomized Controlled Trial." *Psychotherapy Research* 28, no. 2 (2018): 192–202.

Emmons, R. A., and R. Stern. "Gratitude as a Psychotherapeutic Intervention." *Journal of Clinical Psychology* 69, no. 8 (2013): 846–55.

Sirois, F. M., and A. M. Wood. "Gratitude Uniquely Predicts Lower Depression in Chronic Illness Populations: A Longitudinal Study of Inflammatory Bowel Disease and Arthritis." *Health Psychology* 36, no. 2 (2017): 122–32.

Layous, K., K. Sweeny, C. Armenta, S. Na, I. Choi, and S. Lyubomirsky. "The Proximal Experience of Gratitude." *PLoS ONE* 12, no. 7 (2017): e0179123.

Armenta, C., M. Fritz, L. Walsh, and S. Lyubomirsky. "Gratitude and Self-Improvement in Adolescents." Poster presented at the Annual Meeting of the Society for Personality and Social Psychologists, San Antonio, TX, January 2017.

Algoe, S. B., S. L. Gable, and N. C. Maisel. "It's the Little Things: Everyday Gratitude as a Booster Shot for Romantic Relationships." *Personal Relationships* 17, no. 2 (2010): 217–33.

Bartlett, M. Y., P. Condon, J. Cruz, J. Baumann, and D. DeSteno. "Gratitude: Prompting Behaviours That Build Relationships." *Cognition and Emotion* 26, no. 1 (2012): 2–13.

Gordon, A. M., E. A. Impett, A. Kogan, C. Oveis, and D. Keltner. "To Have and to Hold: Gratitude Promotes Relationship Maintenance in Intimate Bonds." *Journal of Personality and Social Psychology* 103, no. 2 (2012): 257–74.

McNulty, J. K., and A. Dugas. "A Dyadic Perspective on Gratitude Sheds Light on Both Its Benefits and Its Costs: Evidence That Low Gratitude Acts as a 'Weak Link.'" *Journal of Family Psychology* 33, no. 7 (2019): 876–81.

Wood, A. M., J. Maltby, R. Gillett, P. A. Linley, and S. Joseph. "The Role of Gratitude in the Development of Social Support, Stress, and Depression: Two Longitudinal Studies." *Journal of Research in Personality* 42, no. 4 (2008): 854–71.

Froh, J. J., C. Yurkewicz, and T. B. Kashdan. "Gratitude and Subjective Well-Being in Early Adolescence: Examining Gender Differences." *Journal of Adolescence* 32, no. 3 (2009): 633–50.

Krause, N., and R. D. Hayward. "Hostility, Religious Involvement, Gratitude, and Self-Rated Health in Late Life." *Research on Aging* 36, no. 6 (2014): 731–52.

Hill, P. L., M. Allemand, and B. W. Roberts. "Examining the Pathways Between Gratitude and Self-Rated Physical Health Across Adulthood." *Personality and Individual Differences* 54, no. 1 (2013): 92–96.

O'Connell, B., D. O'Shea, and S. Gallagher. "Mediating Effects of Loneliness on the Gratitude-Health Link." *Personality and Individual Differences* 98, no. 6 (2016): 179–83.

Emmons, R., and M. E. McCullough. "Counting Blessings Versus Burdens: An Experimental Investigation of Gratitude and Subjective Well-Being in Daily Life." *Journal of Personality and Social Psychology* 84, no. 2 (2003): 377–89.

Mills, P. J., and L. Redwine. "Can Gratitude Be Good for Your Heart?" *Greater Good Magazine.* October 25, 2017. https://greatergood.berkeley.edu/article/item/can_gratitude_be_good_for_your_heart.

Krause, N., R. A. Emmons, G. Ironson, and P. C. Hill. "General Feelings of Gratitude, Gratitude to God, and Hemoglobin A1c: Exploring Variations by Gender." *Journal of Positive Psychology* 12, no. 7 (2017): 639–50.

McCraty, R., M. Atkinson, W. A. Tiller, G. Rein, and A. D. Watkins. "The Effects of Emotions on Short-Term Power Spectrum Analysis of Heart Rate Variability." *American Journal of Cardiology* 76, no. 14 (1995): 1089–93.

Jackowska, M., J. Brown, A. Ronaldson, and A. Steptoe. "The Impact of a Brief Gratitude Intervention on Subjective Well-Being, Biology and Sleep." *Journal of Health Psychology* 21, no. 10 (2016): 2207–17.

Celano, C. M., E. E. Beale, S. R. Beach, A. M. Belcher, L. Suarez, S. R. Motiwala, P. U. Gandhi, H. Gaggin, J. L. Januzzi Jr., B. C. Healy, and J. C. Huffman. "Associations Between Psychological Constructs and Cardiac Biomarkers After Acute Coronary Syndrome." *Psychosomatic Medicine* 79, no. 3 (2017): 318–26.

Wood, A. M., S. Joseph, J. Lloyd, and S. Atkins. "Gratitude Influences Sleep Through the Mechanism of Pre-Sleep Cognitions." *Journal of Psychosomatic Research* 66, no. 1 (2009): 43–48.

Ma, M., J. L. Kibler, and K. Sly. "Gratitude Is Associated with Greater Levels of Protective Factors and Lower Levels of Risks in African American Adolescents." *Journal of Adolescence* 36, no. 5 (2013): 983–91.

Legler, S. R., E. E. Beale, C. M. Celano, S. R. Beach, B. C. Healy, and J. C. Huffman. "State Gratitude for One's Life and Health After an Acute Coronary Syndrome: Prospective Associations with Physical Activity, Medical Adherence, and Re-Hospitalizations." *Journal of Positive Psychology* 14, no. 3 (2019): 283–91.

Millstein, R. A., C. M. Celano, E. E. Beale, S. R. Beach, L. Suarez, A. M. Belcher, J. L. Januzzi, and J. C. Huffman. "The Effects of Optimism and Gratitude on Adherence, Functioning and Mental Health Following an Acute Coronary Syndrome." *General Hospital Psychiatry* 43 (2016): 17–22.

Emmons, R. "Pay It Forward." *Greater Good Magazine.* June 1, 2007. https://greatergood.berkeley.edu/article/item/pay_it_forward.

Bartlett, M. Y., and D. DeSteno. "Gratitude and Prosocial Behavior: Helping When It Costs You." *Psychological Science* 17, no. 4 (2006): 319–25.

Karns, C. M., W. E. Moore III, and U. Mayr. "The Cultivation of Pure Altruism Via Gratitude: A Functional MRI Study of Change with Gratitude Practice." *Frontiers in Human Neuroscience* 11 (2017): 599.

Emmons, R. A., and A. Mishra. "Why Gratitude Enhances Well-Being: What We Know, What We Need to Know." In *Designing Positive Psychology: Taking Stock and Moving Forward,* edited by K. M. Sheldon, T. B. Kashdan, and M. F. Steger, 248–62. New York: Oxford University Press, 2012.

Lambert, N. M., S. M. Graham, F. D. Fincham, and T. F. Stillman. "A Changed Perspective: How Gratitude Can Affect Sense of Coherence Through Positive Reframing." *Journal of Positive Psychology* 4, no. 6 (2009): 461–70.

Froh, J. J., R. A. Emmons, N. A. Card, G. Bono, and J. A. Wilson. "Gratitude and the Reduced Costs of Materialism in Adolescents." *Journal of Happiness Studies* 12, no. 2 (2011): 289–302.

Froh, J. J., G. Bono, and R. Emmons. "Being Grateful Is Beyond Good Manners: Gratitude and Motivation to Contribute to Society Among Early Adolescents." *Motivation and Emotion* 34, no. 2 (2010): 144–57.

Haidt, J. "Wired to Be Inspired." *Greater Good Magazine.* March 1, 2005. https://greatergood.berkeley.edu/article/item/wired_to_be_inspired.

Layous, K., S. K. Nelson, J. L. Kurtz, and S. Lyubomirsky. "What Triggers Prosocial Effort? A Positive Feedback Loop Between Positive Activities, Kindness, and Well-Being." *Journal of Positive Psychology* 12, no. 4 (2017): 385–98.

Kruse, E., J. Chancellor, and S. Lyubomirsky. "State Humility: Measurement, Conceptual Validation, and Intrapersonal Processes." *Self and Identity* 16, no. 4 (2017): 399–438.

Kruse, E., J. Chancellor, P. M. Ruberton, and S. Lyubomirsky. "An Upward Spiral Between Gratitude and Humility." *Social Psychological and Personality Science* 5, no. 7 (2014): 805–14.

Lyubomirsky, S., K. M. Sheldon, and D. Schkade. "Pursuing Happiness: The Architecture of Sustainable Change." *Review of General Psychology* 9, no. 2 (2005): 111–31.

Bonus. How Gratitude Can Help You Achieve Your Goals, by David DeSteno

Excerpted and revised from an article for Greater Good Magazine: *"Three Emotions That Can Help You Succeed at Your Goals," by David DeSteno (January 12, 2018).*

DeSteno, D., Y. Li, L. Dickens, and J. S. Lerner. "Gratitude: A Tool for Reducing Economic Impatience." *Psychological Science* 25, no. 6 (2014): 1262–67.

Dickens, L., and D. DeSteno. "The Grateful Are Patient: Heightened Daily Gratitude Is Associated with Attenuated Temporal Discounting." *Emotion* 16, no. 4 (2016): 421–25.

Estrada, C. A., A. M. Isen, and M. J. Young. "Positive Affect Facilitates Integration of Information and Decreases Anchoring in Reasoning Among Physicians." *Organizational Behavior and Human Decision Processes* 72, no. 1 (1997): 117–35.

Kini, P., J. Wong, S. McInnis, N. Gabana, and J. W. Brown. "The Effects of Gratitude Expression on Neural Activity." *NeuroImage* 128 (2016): 1–10.

Bonus. Can Gratitude Fix Everything? by Kira Newman

Legler, S. R., E. E. Beale, C. M. Celano, S. R. Beach, B. C. Healy, and J. C. Huffman. "State Gratitude for One's Life and Health After an Acute Coronary Syndrome: Prospective Associations with Physical Activity, Medical Adherence, and Re-Hospitalizations." *Journal of Positive Psychology* 14, no. 3 (2019): 283–91.

Emmons, R., and M. E. McCullough. "Counting Blessings Versus Burdens: An Experimental Investigation of Gratitude and Subjective Well-Being in Daily Life." *Journal of Personality and Social Psychology* 84, no. 2 (2003): 377–89.

Chapter 7. How Gender Shapes Gratitude, by Summer Allen

Adapted and revised from an essay for Greater Good Magazine: *"Do Men Have a Gratitude Problem?" by Summer Allen (August 15, 2018).*

Kaplan, J. "Gratitude Survey." Report conducted for the John Templeton Foundation, June–October 2012. https://greatergood.berkeley.edu/ images/uploads/JTF_GRATITUDE_REPORTpub.doc.

Froh, J. J., G. Bono, and R. Emmons. "Being Grateful Is Beyond Good Manners: Gratitude and Motivation to Contribute to Society Among Early Adolescents." *Motivation and Emotion* 34, no. 2 (2010): 144–57.

Froh, J. J., R. A. Emmons, N. A. Card, G. Bono, and J. A. Wilson. "Gratitude and the Reduced Costs of Materialism in Adolescents." *Journal of Happiness Studies* 12, no. 2 (2011): 289–302.

Sun, P., and F. Kong. "Affective Mediators of the Influence of Gratitude on Life Satisfaction in Late Adolescence." *Social Indicators Research* 114, no. 3 (2013): 1361–69.

Kashdan, T. B., A. Mishra, W. E. Breen, and J. J. Froh. "Gender Differences in Gratitude: Examining Appraisals, Narratives, the Willingness to Express Emotions, and Changes in Psychological Needs." *Journal of Personality* 77, no. 3 (2009): 691–730.

Krause, N. "Gratitude Toward God, Stress, and Health in Late Life." *Research on Aging* 28, no. 2 (2006): 163–83.

Sommers, S., and C. Kosmitzki. "Emotion and Social Context: An American-German Comparison." *British Journal of Social Psychology* 27, no. 1 (1988): 35–49.

Smith, J. A. "Should Women Thank Men for Doing the Dishes?" *Greater Good Magazine.* July 5, 2012. https://greatergood.berkeley.edu/article/ item/should_women_thank_men_for_doing_the_dishes.

Kumar, A., and N. Epley. "Undervaluing Gratitude: Expressers Misunderstand the Consequences of Showing Appreciation." *Psychological Science* 29, no. 9 (2018): 1423–35.

Diebel, T., C. Woodcock, C. Cooper, and C. Brignell. "Establishing the Effectiveness of a Gratitude Diary Intervention on Children's Sense of School Belonging." *Educational and Child Psychology* 33, no. 2 (2016): 105–17.

Watkins, P. C., J. Uhder, and S. Pichinevskiy. "Grateful Recounting Enhances Subjective Well-Being: The Importance of Grateful Processing." *Journal of Positive Psychology* 10, no. 2 (2015): 91–98.

Allen, S. "Why Is Gratitude So Hard for Some People?" *Greater Good Magazine.* May 10, 2018. https://greatergood.berkeley.edu/article/item/ why_is_gratitude_so_hard_for_some_people.

Chapter 8. How Cultural Differences Shape Gratitude and Its Impact, by Kira Newman

Revised from an article for Greater Good Magazine: *"How Cultural Differences Shape Your Gratitude," by Kira Newman (July 15, 2019).*

Parks, A. C., and R. Biswas-Diener. "Positive Interventions: Past, Present, and Future." In *Mindfulness, Acceptance, and Positive Psychology: The Seven Foundations of Well-Being,* edited by T. B. Kashdan and J. V. Ciarrochi, 140–65. Oakland, CA: Context Press, 2013.

Farashaiyan, A., and T. K. Hua. "A Cross-Cultural Comparative Study of Gratitude Strategies Between Iranian and Malaysian Postgraduate Students." *Asian Social Science* 8, no. 7 (2012): 139–48.

Mendonça, S. E., E. A. Merçon-Vargas, A. Payir, and J. R. H. Tudge. "The Development of Gratitude in Seven Societies: Cross-Cultural Highlights." *Cross-Cultural Research* 52, no. 1 (2018): 135–50.

Ahar, V., and A. Eslami-Rasekh. "The Effect of Social Status and Size of Imposition on the Gratitude Strategies of Persian and English Speakers." *Journal of Language Teaching and Research* 2, no. 1 (2011): 120–28.

Floyd, S., G. Rossi, J. Baranova, J. Blythe, M. Dingemanse, K. H. Kendrick, J. Zinken, and N. J. Enfield. "Universals and Cultural Diversity in the Expression of Gratitude." *Royal Society Open Science* 5, no. 5 (2018): 180391.

Farashaiyan, A., and K. H. Tan. "A Cross-Cultural Comparative Study of Gratitude Strategies Between Iranian and Malaysian Postgraduate Students." *Asian Social Science* 8, no. 7 (2012): 139–47.

Population Reference Bureau. "2017 World Population Data Sheet." August 2017. https://assets.prb.org/pdf17/2017_World_Population.pdf.

Shen, Y., S. Y. Kim, Y. Wang, and R. K. Chao. "Language Brokering and Adjustment Among Chinese and Korean American Adolescents: A Moderated Mediation Model of Perceived Maternal Sacrifice, Respect for the Mother, and Mother-Child Open Communication." *Asian American Journal of Psychology* 5, no. 2 (2014): 86–95.

Kagitcibasi, C. *Family, Self, and Human Development Across Cultures: Theory and Applications.* New York: Routledge, 2017.

Boehm, J. K., S. Lyubomirsky, and K. M. Sheldon. "A Longitudinal Experimental Study Comparing the Effectiveness of Happiness-Enhancing Strategies in Anglo Americans and Asian Americans." *Cognition and Emotion* 25, no. 7 (2011): 1263–72.

Toepfer, S. M., and K. Walker. "Letters of Gratitude: Improving Well-Being Through Expressive Writing." *Journal of Writing Research* 1, no. 3 (2009): 181–98.

Shin, L. J., C. N. Armenta, S. V. Kamble, S. L. Chang, H. Y. Wu, and S. Lyubomirsky. "Gratitude in Collectivist and Individualist Cultures." *Journal of Positive Psychology* (in press). http://sonjalyubomirsky.com/files/2019/01/Shin-et-al.-in-press.pdf.

Layous, K., H. Lee, I. Choi, and S. Lyubomirsky. "Culture Matters When Designing a Successful Happiness-Increasing Activity: A Comparison of the United States and South Korea." *Journal of Cross-Cultural Psychology* 44, no. 8 (2013): 1294–303.

Kimura, K. "The Multiple Functions of *Sumimasen*." *Issues in Applied Linguistics* 5, no. 2 (1994): 279–302.

Washizu, N., and T. Naito. "The Emotions Sumanai, Gratitude, and Indebtedness, and Their Relations to Interpersonal Orientation and Psychological Well-Being Among Japanese University Students." *International Perspectives in Psychology: Research, Practice, Consultation* 4, no. 3 (2015): 209–22.

Naito, T., and Y. Sakata. "Gratitude, Indebtedness, and Regret on Receiving a Friend's Favor in Japan." *Psychologia* 53, no. 3 (2010): 179–94.

Titova, L., A. E. Wagstaff, and A. C. Parks. "Disentangling the Effects of Gratitude and Optimism: A Cross-Cultural Investigation." *Journal of Cross-Cultural Psychology* 48, no. 5 (2017): 754–70.

Wang, D., Y. C. Wang, and J. R. H. Tudge. "Expressions of Gratitude in Children and Adolescents: Insights from China and the United States." *Journal of Cross-Cultural Psychology* 46, no. 8 (2015): 1039–58.

Chapter 9. How Gratitude Builds Cooperation, by Eric Pedersen and Debra Lieberman

Adapted and revised from an essay for Greater Good Magazine: *"How Gratitude Helps Your Friendships Grow," by Eric Pedersen and Debra Lieberman (December 6, 2017).*

Smith, A., E. J. Pedersen, D. E. Forster, M. E. McCullough, and D. Lieberman. "Cooperation: The Roles of Interpersonal Value and Gratitude." *Evolution and Human Behavior* 38, no. 6 (2017): 695–703.

Forster, D. E., E. J. Pedersen, A. Smith, M. E. McCullough, and D. Lieberman. "Benefit Valuation Predicts Gratitude." *Evolution and Human Behavior* 38, no. 1 (2017): 18–26.

Tooby, J., L. Cosmides, A. Sell, D. Lieberman, and D. Sznycer. "Internal Regulatory Variables and the Design of Human Motivation: A Computational and Evolutionary Approach." In *Handbook of Approach and Avoidance Motivation,* edited by A. Elliot, 251–71. Mahwah, NJ: Lawrence Erlbaum Associates, 2008.

Lieberman, D., J. Tooby, and L. Cosmides. "The Architecture of Human Kin Detection." *Nature* 445, no. 7129 (2007): 727–31.

Part 3. How to Be Grateful

Chapter 10. How to Cultivate Gratitude in Yourself, by Jeremy Adam Smith

Adapted and revised from an essay for Greater Good Magazine: *"Six Habits of Highly Grateful People," by Jeremy Adam Smith (August 4, 2017).*

Carter, C. "Habits Are Everything." *Greater Good Magazine.* April 16, 2012. https://greatergood.berkeley.edu/article/item/habits1.

Emmons, R. "How Gratitude Can Help You Through Hard Times." *Greater Good Magazine.* May 13, 2013. https://greatergood.berkeley.edu/article/item/how_gratitude_can_help_you_through_hard_times.

Frias, A., P. C. Watkins, A. C. Webber, and J. J. Froh. "Death and Gratitude: Death Reflection Enhances Gratitude." *Journal of Positive Psychology* 6, no. 2 (2011): 154–162.

Koo, M., S. B. Algoe, T. D. Wilson, and D. T. Gilbert. "It's a Wonderful Life: Mentally Subtracting Positive Events Improves People's Affective States, Contrary to Their Affective Forecasts." *Journal of Personality and Social Psychology* 95, no. 5 (2008): 1217–24.

Quoidbach, J., and E. Dunn. "Give It Up: A Strategy for Combating Hedonic Adaptation." *Social Psychological and Personality Science* 4, no. 5 (2013): 563–68.

Bryant, F. B. *Savoring: A New Model of Positive Experience.* Abingdon, UK: Routledge, 2006.

Nauman, E. "Do Rituals Help Us to Savor Food?" *Greater Good Magazine.* August 7, 2013. https://greatergood.berkeley.edu/article/item/do_rituals_help_us_to_savor_food.

Vohs, K. D., Y. Wang, F. Gino, and M. I. Norton. "Rituals Enhance Consumption." *Psychological Science* 24, no. 9 (2013): 1714–21.

Lyubomirsky, S., and J. Marsh. "Debunking the Myths of Happiness." *Greater Good Magazine.* February 20, 2013. https://greatergood.berkeley.edu/article/item/sonja_lyubomirsky_on_the_myths_of_happiness.

Emmons, R. "What Gets in the Way of Gratitude?" *Greater Good Magazine.* November 12, 2013. https://greatergood.berkeley.edu/article/item/what_stops_gratitude.

Gordon, A. "Four Ways to Make the Most of Gratitude on Valentine's Day." *Greater Good Magazine.* February 12, 2013. https://greatergood.berkeley

.edu/article/item/four_ways_to_make_the_most_of_gratitude_on
_valentines_day.

Bonus. How to Make the Most of Your Gratitude Journal, by Alex Springer and Jason Marsh

Adapted and revised from two essays for Greater Good Magazine: *"Five Ways to Make the Most of Your Gratitude," by Alex Springer (January 22, 2018), and "Tips for Keeping a Gratitude Journal," by Jason Marsh (November 17, 2011).*

Emmons, R. A., and M. E. McCullough. "Counting Blessings Versus Burdens: An Experimental Investigation of Gratitude and Subjective Well-Being in Daily Life." *Journal of Personality and Social Psychology* 84, no. 2 (2003): 377–89.

Bonus. When Gratitude Exercises Feel Bad, by Megan M. Fritz and Sonja Lyubomirsky

Adapted and revised from an essay for Greater Good Magazine: *"When Happiness Exercises Don't Make You Happier," by Megan Fritz and Sonja Lyubomirsky (July 27, 2018).*

Armenta, C. N., M. M. Fritz, and S. Lyubomirsky. "Functions of Positive Emotions: Gratitude as a Motivator of Self-Improvement and Positive Change." *Emotion Review* (2016): 1–8.

Nelson, K. S., and S. Lyubomirsky. "Finding Happiness: Tailoring Positive Activities for Optimal Well-Being Benefits." In *Handbook of Positive Emotions,* edited by M. Tugade, M. Shiota, and L. Kirby. New York: Guilford Press, 2012.

Bonus. Five Ways Giving Thanks Can Backfire, by Amie Gordon

Adapted and revised from an essay for Greater Good Magazine: *"Five Ways Giving Thanks Can Backfire," by Amie Gordon (April 29, 2013).*

Marsh, J. "Tips for Keeping a Gratitude Journal." *Greater Good Magazine.* November 17, 2011. https://greatergood.berkeley.edu/article/item/ tips_for_keeping_a_gratitude_journal.

Armenta, C., M. Fritz, L. Walsh, and S. Lyubomirsky. "Gratitude and Self-Improvement in Adolescents." Poster presented at the Annual Meeting of the Society for Personality and Social Psychologists, San Antonio, TX, January 2017.

Chapter 11. How to Say Thanks Without Feeling Indebted, by Jill Suttie

Adapted and revised from an essay for Greater Good Magazine: *"How to Say Thanks Without Feeling Indebted," by Jill Suttie (November 23, 2016).*

Watkins, P., J. Scheer, M. Ovnicek, and R. Kolts. "The Debt of Gratitude: Dissociating Gratitude and Indebtedness." *Cognition and Emotion* 20, no. 2 (2006): 217–41.

Algoe, S. B., S. L. Gable, and N. C. Maisel. "It's the Little Things: Everyday Gratitude as a Booster Shot for Romantic Relationships." *Personal Relationships* 17, no. 2 (2010): 217–33.

Tsang, J. A. "Gratitude for Small and Large Favors: A Behavioral Test." *Journal of Positive Psychology* 2, no. 3 (2007): 157–67.

Pelser, J., K. de Ruyter, M. Wetzels, D. Grewal, D. Cox, and J. van Beuningen. "B2B Channel Partner Programs: Disentangling Indebtedness from Gratitude." *Journal of Retailing* 91, no. 4 (2015): 660–78.

Hitokoto, H. "Indebtedness in Cultural Context: The Role of Culture in the Felt Obligation to Reciprocate." *Asian Journal of Social Psychology* 19, no. 1 (2016): 16–25.

Mathews, M. A., and J. D. Green. "Looking at Me, Appreciating You: Self-Focused Attention Distinguishes Between Gratitude and Indebtedness." *Cognition and Emotion* 24, no. 4 (2010): 710–18.

Mathews, M. A., and N. J. Shook. "Promoting or Preventing Thanks: Regulatory Focus and Its Effect on Gratitude and Indebtedness." *Journal of Research in Personality* 47, no. 3 (2013): 191–95.

Delvaux, E., N. Vanbeselaere, and B. Mesquita. "Dynamic Interplay Between Norms and Experiences of Anger and Gratitude in Groups." *Small Group Research* 46, no. 3 (2015): 300–23.

Froh, J. J., G. Bono, J. Fan, R. A. Emmons, K. Henderson, C. Harris, H. Leggio, and A. M. Wood. "Nice Thinking! An Educational Intervention That Teaches Children to Think Gratefully." *School Psychology Review* 43, no. 2 (2014): 132–52.

Dunn, E., and M. Norton. "How to Make Giving Feel Good." *Greater Good Magazine.* June 18, 2013. https://greatergood.berkeley.edu/article/item/how_to_make_giving_feel_good.

Algoe, S. B., J. Haidt, and S. L. Gable. "Beyond Reciprocity: Gratitude and Relationships in Everyday Life." *Emotion* 8, no. 3 (2008): 425–29.

Kennelly, S. "10 Steps to Savoring the Good Things in Life." *Greater Good Magazine.* July 23, 2012. https://greatergood.berkeley.edu/article/item/10_steps_to_savoring_the_good_things_in_life.

Semple, R. J. "Does Mindfulness Meditation Enhance Attention? A Randomized Controlled Trial." *Mindfulness* 1 (2010): 121–30.

Matvienko-Sikar, K., and S. Dockray. "The Effects of Two Novel Gratitude and Mindfulness Interventions on Well-Being." *Journal of Alternative and Complementary Medicine* 21, no. 4 (2015): 1–3.

Chapter 12. Can Loss Make You More Grateful? by Nathan Greene

Based on an article originally published in Elephant Journal *(November 6, 2017) and revised for* Greater Good Magazine: *"Can Losing a Loved One Make You More Grateful?" by Nathan Greene (March 22, 2018).*

Frias, A., P. C. Watkins, A. C. Webber, and J. J. Froh. "Death and Gratitude: Death Reflection Enhances Gratitude." *Journal of Positive Psychology* 6, no. 2 (2011): 154–62.

King, L. A., J. A. Hicks, and J. Abdelkhalik. "Death, Life, Scarcity, and Value: An Alternative Perspective on the Meaning of Death." *Psychological Science* 20, no. 12 (2009): 1459–62.

Greene, N., and K. McGovern. "Gratitude, Psychological Well-Being, and Perceptions of Posttraumatic Growth in Adults Who Lost a Parent in Childhood." *Death Studies* 41, no. 7 (2017): 436–46.

Bonus. Grief, Grace, and Gratitude, by Arianna Huffington

Adapted from Thrive: The Third Metric to Redefining Success and Creating a Life of Well-Being, Wisdom, and Wonder, *by Arianna Huffington (Harmony, 2014); this essay was originally published in* Greater Good Magazine: *"Can Gratitude Help You Thrive?" by Arianna Huffington (April 15, 2014).*

John-Roger and P. Kaye. *The Rest of Your Life: Finding Repose in the Beloved.* Chicago: Mandeville Press, 2007.

Chapter 13. How Gratitude Can Help You Through Hard Times, by Robert Emmons

Adapted and revised from an essay for Greater Good Magazine: *"How Gratitude Can Help You Through Hard Times," by Robert Emmons (May 13, 2013).*

Emmons, R. *Gratitude Works! A 21-Day Program for Creating Emotional Prosperity.* San Francisco, CA: Jossey-Bass, 2013.

Watkins, P. C., L. Cruz, H. Holben, and R. L. Kolts. "Taking Care of Business? Grateful Processing of Unpleasant Memories." *Journal of Positive Psychology* 3, no. 2 (2008): 87–99.

Part 4. How to Be a Grateful Family

Chapter 14. Why Couples Need to Thank to Each Other, by Jess Alberts and Angela Trethewey

Revised from an essay for Greater Good Magazine: *"Love, Honor, and Thank," by Jess Alberts and Angela Trethewey (June 1, 2007).*

Cowan, C. P., and P. A. Cowan. *When Partners Become Parents: The Big Life Change for Couples.* Mahwah, NJ: Lawrence Erlbaum Associates, 2000.

Hochschild, A. R., and A. Machung. *The Second Shift*. New York: Penguin Books, 2003.

Alberts, J., S. Tracy, and A. Trethewey. "An Integrative Theory of the Division of Domestic Labor: Threshold Level, Social Organizing and Sensemaking." *Journal of Family Communication* 11, no. 1 (2011): 21–38.

Hochschild, A. R. *The Managed Heart Commercialization of Human Feeling*. Updated ed. Berkeley: University of California Press, 2012.

Holbrook, C. T., R. M. Clark, R. Jeanson, S. M. Bertram, P. F. Kukuk, and J. H. Fewell. "Emergence and Consequences of Division of Labor in Associations of Normally Solitary Sweat Bees." *Ethology* 115, no. 4 (2009): 301–10.

Bonus. How to Say Thank-You to Your Partner, by Sara Algoe

Excerpted and revised from an essay for Greater Good Magazine: *"How to Say 'Thank You' to Your Partner," by Sara Algoe (February 27, 2018).*

Algoe, S. B., and R. Zhaoyang. "Positive Psychology in Context: Effects of Expressing Gratitude in Ongoing Relationships Depend on Perceptions of Enactor Responsiveness." *Journal of Positive Psychology* 11, no. 4 (2015): 399–415.

Algoe, S. B., L. E. Kurtz, and N. M. Hilaire. "Putting the 'You' in 'Thank You': Examining Other-Praising Behavior as the Active Relational Ingredient in Expressed Gratitude." *Social Psychological and Personality Science* 7, no. 7 (2016): 658–66.

Bonus. Why Men Need to Learn Gratitude, by Jeremy Adam Smith

Excerpted and revised from an essay for Greater Good Magazine: *"Should Women Thank Men for Doing the Dishes?" by Jeremy Adam Smith (July 5, 2012).*

Cho, Y., and N. J. Fast. "Power, Defensive Denigration, and the Assuaging Effect of Gratitude Expression." *Journal of Experimental Social Psychology* 48, no. 3 (2012): 778–82.

Inesi, M. E., D. H. Gruenfeld, and A. D. Galinsky. "How Power Corrupts Relationships: Cynical Attributions for Others' Generous Acts." *Journal of Experimental Social Psychology* 48, no. 4 (2012): 795–803.

Gordon, A. M. "Beyond 'Thanks': Power as a Determinant of Gratitude." PhD diss., University of California, Berkeley, 2013. https://pdfs.semanticscholar.org/3660/755a13703f3a65b7de9827b11b4f1136a951.pdf.

Bonus. How Gratitude Can Help Couples Through Illness, by Jill Suttie

Excerpted and revised from an essay for Greater Good Magazine: *"Can Gratitude Help Couples Through Hard Times?" by Jill Suttie (May 24, 2018).*

Kindt, S., M. Vansteenkiste, T. Loeys, A. Cano, E. Lauwerier, L. L. Verhofstadt, and L. Goubert. "When Is Helping Your Partner with Chronic Pain a Burden? The Relation Between Helping Motivation and Personal and Relational Functioning." *Pain Medicine* 16, no. 9 (2015): 1732–44.

Kindt, S., M. Vansteenkiste, T. Loeys, and L. Goubert. "Helping Motivation and Well-Being of Chronic Pain Couples." *Pain* 157, no. 7 (2016): 1551–62.

Algoe, S. B., B. L. Fredrickson, and S. L. Gable. "The Social Functions of the Emotion of Gratitude via Expression." *Emotion* 13, no. 4 (2013): 605–9.

Miller, L. R., A. Cano, and L. H. Wurm. "A Motivational Therapeutic Assessment Improves Pain, Mood, and Relationship Satisfaction in Couples with Chronic Pain." *The Journal of Pain* 14, no. 5 (2013): 525–37.

Kindt, S., M. Vansteenkiste, A. Cano, and L. Goubert. "When Is Your Partner Willing to Help You? The Role of Daily Goal Conflict and Perceived Gratitude." *Motivation and Emotion* 41, no. 6 (2017): 671–82.

Chapter 15. How to Help Gratitude Grow in Your Kids, by Maryam Abdullah

Revised from an essay for Greater Good Magazine: *"How to Help Gratitude Grow in Your Kids," by Maryam Abdullah (March 13, 2018).*

Halberstadt, A. G., H. A. Langley, A. M. Hussong, W. A. Rothenberg, J. L. Coffman, I. Mokrova, and P. R. Costanzo. "Parents' Understanding of Gratitude in Children: A Thematic Analysis." *Early Childhood Research Quarterly* 36 (February 2016): 439–51.

Greater Good Science Center. "What Is Gratitude?" *Greater Good Magazine.* Accessed November 19, 2019. https://greatergood.berkeley.edu/topic/gratitude/definition.

Rothenberg, W. A., A. M. Hussong, H. A. Langley, G. A. Egerton, A. G. Halberstadt, J. L. Coffman, I. Mokrova, and P. R. Costanzo. "Grateful Parents Raising Grateful Children: Niche Selection and the Socialization of Child Gratitude." *Applied Developmental Science* 21, no. 2 (2016): 106–20.

Morgan, B., and L. Gulliford. "Assessing Influences on Gratitude Experience." In *Developing Gratitude in Children and Adolescent,* edited by J. Tudge and L. Freitas, 65–88. New York: Cambridge University Press, 2017.

Greater Good Science Center. "Feeling Supported." Greater Good in Action. Accessed November 19, 2019. https://ggia.berkeley.edu/practice/feeling_supported.

————. "Three Good Things." Greater Good in Action. Accessed November 19, 2019. https://ggia.berkeley.edu/practice/three-good-things.

————. "Gratitude Meditation." Greater Good in Action. Accessed November 19, 2019. https://ggia.berkeley.edu/practice/gratitude_meditation.

Hussong, A. M., H. A. Langley, W. A. Rothenberg, J. L. Coffman, A. G. Halberstadt, P. R. Costanzo, and I. Mokrova. "Raising Grateful Children One Day at a Time." *Applied Developmental Science* 23, no. 4 (2018): 371–84.

Chapter 16. Feeling Entitled to a Little Gratitude on Mother's Day? by Christine Carter

Revised from an essay for Greater Good Magazine: *"Feeling Entitled to a Little Gratitude on Mother's Day?" by Christine Carter (May 3, 2016).*

Algoe, S. B. "Find, Remind, and Bind: The Functions of Gratitude in Everyday Relationships." *Social and Personality Psychology Compass* 6, no. 6 (2012): 455–69.

Carter, C. "Friday Inspiration: The Mother's Day Note You Deserve." *Christine Carter* (blog), March 18, 2014. https://www.christinecarter.com/2014/05/friday-inspiration-the-mothers-day-note-you-deserve.

Carter, C. "My Love-Hate Relationship with Mother's Day." *Christine Carter* (blog). May 20, 2013. https://www.christinecarter.com/2013/05/my-love-hate-relationship-with-mothers-day.

Horowitz, J. M. "Who Does More at Home When Both Parents Work? Depends on Which One You Ask." *FactTank* (blog). November 5, 2015. https://www.pewresearch.org/fact-tank/2015/11/05/who-does-more-at-home-when-both-parents-work-depends-on-which-one-you-ask.

Chapter 17. What Being a Stepfather Taught Me About Gratitude, by Jeremy Adam Smith

Adapted and revised from an essay for Greater Good Magazine: *"What Being a Stepfather Taught Me About Love," by Jeremy Adam Smith (June 12, 2019).*

Gold, J. M. "Helping Stepfathers 'Step Away' from the Role of 'Father': Directions for Family Intervention." *The Family Journal* 18, no. 2 (2010): 208–14.

Nelson, M. *The Argonauts.* Minneapolis: Graywolf Press, 2016.

Carter, C. "How to Fight." *Greater Good Magazine.* February 11, 2008. https://greatergood.berkeley.edu/article/item/how_to_fight.

Greater Good Science Center. "What Is Forgiveness?" *Greater Good Magazine.* Accessed November 19, 2019. https://greatergood.berkeley. .edu/topic/forgiveness/definition#what-is-forgiveness.

———. "Making an Effective Apology." Greater Good in Action. Accessed November 19, 2019. https://ggia.berkeley.edu/practice/ making_an_effective_apology.

———. "What Is Compassion?" *Greater Good Magazine.* Accessed November 19, 2019. https://greatergood.berkeley.edu/topic/compassion/ definition#what-is-compassion.

———. "What Is Happiness?" *Greater Good Magazine.* Accessed November 19, 2019. https://greatergood.berkeley.edu/topic/happiness/ definition#what-is-happiness.

Marsh, J., and J. Suttie. "Is a Happy Life Different from a Meaningful One?" *Greater Good Magazine.* February 25, 2014. https://greatergood.berkeley. edu/article/item/happy_life_different_from_meaningful_life.

Part 5. How to Foster Gratefulness Around You

Chapter 18. How to Foster Gratitude in Schools, by Jeffrey Froh and Giacomo Bono

Revised from an essay for Greater Good Magazine: *"How to Foster Gratitude in Schools," by Jeffrey Froh and Giacomo Bono (November 19, 2012).*

Froh, J. J., W. J. Sefick, and R. A. Emmons. "Counting Blessings in Early Adolescents: An Experimental Study of Gratitude and Subjective Well-Being." *Journal of School Psychology* 46, no. 2 (2007): 213–33.

Froh, J. J., T. B. Kashdan, K. M. Ozimkowski, and N. Miller. "Who Benefits the Most from a Gratitude Intervention in Children and Adolescents? Examining Positive Affect as a Moderator." *Journal of Positive Psychology* 4, no. 5 (2009): 408–22.

Chapter 19. Gratitude Is a Survival Skill, by Shawn Taylor

Revised from an essay for Greater Good Magazine: *"Gratitude Is a Survival Skill," by Shawn Taylor (June 12, 2018).*

Chapter 20. Five Ways to Cultivate Gratitude at Work, by Jeremy Adam Smith and Kira Newman

Adapted and revised from two essays for Greater Good Magazine: *"Five Ways to Cultivate Gratitude at Work," by Jeremy Adam Smith (May 16, 2013), and "How Gratitude Can Transform Your Workplace," by Kira Newman (September 6, 2017).*

Kaplan, J. "Gratitude Survey." Report conducted for the John Templeton Foundation, June–October 2012. https://greatergood.berkeley.edu/ images/uploads/JTF_GRATITUDE_REPORTpub.doc.

Grant, A. M., and F. Gino. "A Little Thanks Goes a Long Way: Explaining Why Gratitude Expressions Motivate Prosocial Behavior." *Journal of Personality and Social Psychology* 98, no. 6 (2010): 946–55.

Simon-Thomas, E. R. "A 'Thnx' a Day Keeps the Doctor Away." *Greater Good Magazine*. December 19, 2012. https://greatergood.berkeley.edu /article/item/a_thnx_a_day_keeps_the_doctor_away.

Chapman, G. *The Five Love Languages: How to Express Heartfelt Commitment to Your Mate.* Chicago: Northfield Publishing, 1995.

Bonus. What Does a Grateful Organization Look Like?
by Emily Nauman

Excerpted from an essay for Greater Good Magazine: "What Does a Grateful Organization Look Like?" by Emily Nauman (February 26, 2014).

Greater Good Science Center. "Expanding the Science and Practice of Gratitude." Accessed November 19, 2019. https://ggsc.berkeley.edu/ what_we_do/major_initiatives/expanding_gratitude.

———. "Grateful Organizations Quiz." *Greater Good Magazine.* Accessed November 19, 2019. https://greatergood.berkeley.edu/quizzes/take_quiz/ grateful_organizations.

Bonus. Gratitude as a Pathway to Positive Emotions at Work,
by Kira Newman

Excerpted from an essay for Greater Good Magazine: "How Gratitude Can Transform Your Workplace," by Kira Newman (September 6, 2017).

Ovans, A. "How Emotional Intelligence Became a Key Leadership Skill." *Harvard Business Review.* April 28, 2015. https://hbr.org/2015/04/ how-emotional-intelligence-became-a-key-leadership-skill.

Krznaric, R. "Six Habits of Highly Empathic People." *Greater Good Magazine.* November 27, 2012. https://greatergood.berkeley.edu/article/item/ six_habits_of_highly_empathic_people1.

Suttie, J. "Compassionate Across Cubicles." *Greater Good Magazine.* March 1, 2006. https://greatergood.berkeley.edu/article/item/ compassion_across_cubicles/.

Deterline, B. "The Power of Forgiveness at Work." *Greater Good Magazine.* August 26, 2016. https://greatergood.berkeley.edu/article/item/ the_power_of_forgiveness_at_work.

Titova, L., A. E. Wagstaff, and A. C. Parks. "Disentangling the Effects of Gratitude and Optimism: A Cross-Cultural Investigation." *Journal of Cross-Cultural Psychology* 48, no. 5 (2017): 754–70.

Andersson, L. M., R. A. Giacalone, and C. L. Jurkiewicz. "On the Relationship of Hope and Gratitude to Corporate Social Responsibility." *Journal of Business Ethics* 70, no. 4 (2006): 401–9.

Spence, J. R., D. J. Brown, L. M. Keeping, and H. Lian. "Helpful Today, But Not Tomorrow? Feeling Grateful as a Predictor of Daily Organizational Citizenship Behaviors." *Personnel Psychology* 67, no. 3 (2014): 705–38.

Chapter 21. Why Health Professionals Should Cultivate Gratitude, by Leif Hass

Adapted and revised from an essay for Greater Good Magazine: *"Why Health Professionals Should Cultivate Gratitude," by Leif Hass (July 26, 2017).*

Wood, A. M., J. J. Froh, and A. W. A. Geraghty. "Gratitude and Well-Being: A Review and Theoretical Integration." *Clinical Psychology Review* 30, no. 7 (2010): 890–905.

Redwine, L. S., B. L. Henry, M. A. Pung, K. Wilson, K. Chinh, B. Knight, S. Jain, et al. "Pilot Randomized Study of a Gratitude Journaling Intervention on Heart Rate Variability and Inflammatory Biomarkers in Patients with Stage B Heart Failure." *Psychosomatic Medicine* 78, no. 6 (2016): 667–76.

Advisory Board. "Physician Burnout in 2019, Charted." January 18, 2019. https://www.advisory.com/daily-briefing/2019/01/18/burnout-report.

Jerath, R., J. W. Edry, V. A. Barnes, and V. Jerath. "Physiology of Long Pranayamic Breathing: Neural Respiratory Elements May Provide a Mechanism That Explains How Slow Deep Breathing Shifts the Autonomic Nervous System." *Medical Hypotheses* 67, no. 3 (2006): 566–71.

Norman, G. J., J. T. Cacioppo, J. S. Morris, W. B. Malarkey, G. G. Berntson, and A. C. Devries. "Oxytocin Increases Autonomic Cardiac Control: Moderation by Loneliness." *Biological Psychology* 86, no. 3 (2010): 174–80.

Cheng, S. T., P. K. Tsui, and J. H. Lam. "Improving Mental Health in Health Care Practitioners: Randomized Controlled Trial of a Gratitude Intervention." *Journal of Consulting and Clinical Psychology* 83, no. 1 (2015): 177–86.

Bartlett, M. Y., and D. Desteno. "Gratitude and Prosocial Behavior: Helping When It Costs You." *Psychological Science* 17, no. 4 (2006): 319–25.

Bonus. How One Provider Is Fostering Gratitude in Health Care, by Catherine Brozena

Excerpted from an essay for Greater Good Magazine: *"How Gratitude Can Reduce Burnout in Health Care," by Catherine Brozena (January 11, 2018).*

Chapter 22. How to Help Other People Become More Grateful, by Tom Gilovich

Adapted and revised from an essay for Greater Good Magazine: *"How to Overcome the Biggest Obstacle to Gratitude," by Tom Gilovich (December 12, 2017).*

Walker, J., A. Kumar, and T. Gilovich. "Cultivating Gratitude and Giving Through Experiential Consumption." *Emotion* 16, no. 8 (2016): 1126–36.

Carter, T. J., and T. Gilovich. "I Am What I Do, Not What I Have: The Differential Centrality of Experiential and Material Purchases to the Self." *Journal of Personality and Social Psychology* 102, no. 6 (2012): 1304–17.

Kumar, A., and T. Gilovich. "Some 'Thing' to Talk About? Differential Story Utility from Experiential and Material Purchases." *Personality and Social Psychology Bulletin* 41, no. 10 (2015): 1320–31.

Part 6. Conversations About the Transformative Potential of Gratitude

Chapter 23. Can Gratitude Confront Suffering? A Conversation with Jack Kornfield, by Jill Suttie

Originally published in Greater Good Magazine: *"Why We Should Seek Happiness Even in Hard Times," by Jill Suttie (January 4, 2019).*

Bonus. Can Gratitude Make Society More Trusting? by Elizabeth Hopper

Excerpted and revised from an article for Greater Good Magazine: *"Can Gratitude Make Society More Trusting?" by Elizabeth Hopper (June 13, 2017).*

Smith, J. A., and P. Paxton. "America's Trust Fall." *Greater Good Magazine.* September 1, 2008. https://greatergood.berkeley.edu/article/item/americas_trust_fall.

Gottman, J. "The Importance of Trust." *Greater Good Magazine.* October 2011. https://greatergood.berkeley.edu/gg_live/science_meaningful_life_videos/speaker/john_gottman/the_importance_of_trust.

Drazkowski, D., L. D. Kaczmarek, and T. B. Kashdan. "Gratitude Pays: A Weekly Gratitude Intervention Influences Monetary Decisions,

Physiological Responses, and Emotional Experiences During a Trust-Related Social Interaction." *Personality and Individual Differences* 110 (May 2017): 148–53.

Bonus. Can Gratitude Beat Materialism? by Dacher Keltner and Jason Marsh

Excerpted and revised from an article for Greater Good Magazine: *"How Gratitude Beats Materialism," by Jason Marsh and Dacher Keltner (January 8, 2015).*

Richins, M. L., and S. Dawson. "A Consumer Values Orientation for Materialism and Its Measurement: Scale Development and Validation." *Journal of Consumer Research* 19, no. 3 (1992): 303–16.

Kashdan, T. B., and W. E. Breen. "Materialism and Diminished Well-Being: Experiential Avoidance as a Mediating Mechanism." *Journal of Social and Clinical Psychology* 26, no. 5 (2007): 521–39.

Tsang, J. A., T. P. Carpenter, J. A. Roberts, M. B. Frisch, and R. D. Carlisle. "Why Are Materialists Less Happy? The Role of Gratitude and Need Satisfaction in the Relationship Between Materialism and Life Satisfaction." *Personality and Individual Differences* 64 (July 2014): 62–66.

Lambert, N. M., F. D. Fincham, T. F. Stillman, and L. R. Dean. "More Gratitude, Less Materialism: The Mediating Role of Life Satisfaction." *Journal of Positive Psychology* 4, no. 1 (2009): 32–42.

Chapter 24. Can Gratitude Bring Americans Back Together? A Conversation with W. Kamau Bell, by Jeremy Adam Smith

Originally published in Greater Good Magazine: *"W. Kamau Bell's United Thanks of America," by Jeremy Adam Smith (November 14, 2018).*

Bonus. Gratitude Encourages Voting, by Jill Suttie

Excerpted and revised from an article for Greater Good Magazine: *"The Emotions That Make You Decide to Vote," by Jill Suttie (October 31, 2018).*

Panagopoulos, C. "Thank You for Voting: Gratitude Expression and Voter Mobilization." *The Journal of Politics* 73, no. 3 (2011): 707–17.

Chapter 25. Is Gratitude the Path to a Better World? A Conversation with Brother David Steindl-Rast, by Jill Suttie

Originally published in Greater Good Magazine: *"Is Gratitude the Path to a Better World?" by Jill Suttie (May 29, 2013).*

Editor **Jeremy Adam Smith** edits the Greater Good Science Center's online magazine, *Greater Good*. He is author of *The Daddy Shift*, and coeditor of three anthologies. His coverage of racial and economic segregation in San Francisco, CA, schools has won numerous honors, including the Sigma Delta Chi Award for investigative reporting, and he is a three-time winner of the John Swett Award from the California Teachers Association.

Smith's articles and essays have appeared in the *San Francisco Chronicle*, *Scientific American*, *Utne Reader*, *The Nation*, *Mindful*, *Wired*, and many other periodicals, websites, and books. Jeremy has also been interviewed by *The Today Show*, *The New York Times*, *USA TODAY*, *Working Mother*, *Nightline*, ABC News, NBC News, *The Globe and Mail*, and numerous NPR shows about parenting and education. Before joining the Greater Good Science Center, Jeremy was a 2010–2011 John S. Knight Journalism Fellow at Stanford University.

Editor **Kira M. Newman** is managing editor of *Greater Good* magazine, and a former course assistant for The Science of Happiness online course on edX. Her work has been published in a variety of outlets, including *The Washington Post*, *HuffPost*, *Social Media Monthly*, and *Mindful* magazine. She has created large communities around the science of happiness, including the online course, The Year of Happy; and the CaféHappy meetup in Toronto, ON, Canada. Previously, she was a technology journalist and editor for *Tech.Co*.

Editor **Jason Marsh** is founding editor in chief of *Greater Good* magazine, and the Greater Good Science Center's director of programs. He is also coeditor of two anthologies of *Greater Good* articles: *The Compassionate Instinct* and *Are We Born Racist?* His writing has also appeared in *The Wall Street Journal*, the *San Francisco Chronicle*, and *Utne Reader*, among other publications, and he writes regularly for the opinion section of CNN.com.

Editor **Dacher Keltner, PhD**, is founding director of the Greater Good Science Center, and a professor of psychology at the University of California, Berkeley. He is author of *The Power Paradox* and *Born to Be Good*, and coeditor of *The Compassionate Instinct*.

Real change *is* possible

For more than forty-five years, New Harbinger has published proven-effective self-help books and pioneering workbooks to help readers of all ages and backgrounds improve mental health and well-being, and achieve lasting personal growth. In addition, our spirituality books offer profound guidance for deepening awareness and cultivating healing, self-discovery, and fulfillment.

Founded by psychologist Matthew McKay and Patrick Fanning, New Harbinger is proud to be an independent, employee-owned company. Our books reflect our core values of integrity, innovation, commitment, sustainability, compassion, and trust. Written by leaders in the field and recommended by therapists worldwide, New Harbinger books are practical, accessible, and provide real tools for real change.

 **newharbinger**publications